SCRIBBLE SCRIBBLE
Early Writing Skills

by Marilynn G. Barr

LAB20132
SCRIBBLE SCRIBBLE
by Marilynn G. Barr

Published by: Little Acorn Books™
Originally published by: Monday Morning Books, Inc.

Entire contents copyright © 2013 Little Acorn Books™

Little Acorn Books
PO Box 8787
Greensboro, NC 27419-0787

Promoting Early Skills for a Lifetime™

Little Acorn Books™
is an imprint of Little Acorn Associates, Inc.

http://www.littleacornbooks.com

Permission is hereby granted to reproduce student materials in this book for non-commercial individual or classroom use. *School-wide or system-wide use is expressly prohibited.

ISBN 978-1-937257-19-4

Printed in the United States of America

Scribble Scribble

Contents

Introduction.. 4
   Writing Practice Pages
   Learning About Letters Book
   Scribble Scribble Picture Books
   Connect-the-Letters, Connect-the-Numbers
   Scribble Scribble Finger Puppets and Props

Scribble, Scribble Letters
   Learning About Letter Aa 5
   Learning About Letter Bb 6
   Learning About Letter Cc...................... 7
   Learning About Letter Dd 8
   Learning About Letter Ee...................... 9
   Learning About Letter Ff......................10
   Learning About Letter Gg 11
   Learning About Letter Hh.....................12
   Learning About Letter Ii......................13
   Learning About Letter Jj......................14
   Learning About Letter Kk.....................15
   Learning About Letter Ll......................16
   Learning About Letter Mm.....................17
   Learning About Letter Nn.....................18
   Learning About Letter Oo.....................19
   Learning About Letter Pp.....................20
   Learning About Letter Qq.....................21
   Learning About Letter Rr.....................22
   Learning About Letter Ss.....................23
   Learning About Letter Tt.....................24
   Learning About Letter Uu 25
   Learning About Letter Vv.....................26
   Learning About Letter Ww 27
   Learning About Letter Xx....................28
   Learning About Letter Yy.....................29
   Learning About Letter Zz 30

Scribble, Scribble Numbers
   Learning About Number 1......................31
   Learning About Number 2 32
   Learning About Number 3 33
   Learning About Number 4 34
   Learning About Number 5 35
   Learning About Number 6 36
   Learning About Number 7 37
   Learning About Number 8 38
   Learning About Number 9 39
   Learning About Number 10 40

Connect-the-Letters
   Connect-the-Letters (a-m).................41
   Connect-the-Letters (n-z)..................43
   Connect-the-Letters (A-M) 45
   Connect-the-Letters (N-Z)..................47
   Connect-the-Letters (a-z)..................49
   Connect-the-Letters (A-Z)..................51

Connect-the-Numbers
   Connect-the-Numbers (1-10)................54
   Connect-the-Numbers (1-20) 59

Scribble Scribble Book Pages....................64

Scribble Scribble Introduction

Scribble Scribble features hands-on readiness and writing skills practice. Children practice fine motor skills while learning about letters and numbers. Every activity page includes a writing strip, letter or number shape pictures, and a picture book page. Children practice tracing letters or numerals on writing strips. Letter shape pictures display three beginning sound pictures for language skills development. Number shape pictures include numerals, number words, and number sets for additional number skills practice. Easy-to-follow directions offer advanced learners reading practice. Nonreaders can complete activity sheets with oral direction. Provide children with crayons to trace and color each activity.

Writing Practice Pages

Have children trace, color, cut out, and glue each writing strip on a Writing Practice Page (p. 64). Form a book with each child's set of writing practice pages. Cut construction paper covers for children to decorate. Write "I Can Write Letters" or "I Can Write Numbers" on the covers. Staple each child's cover and set of writing practice pages in order.

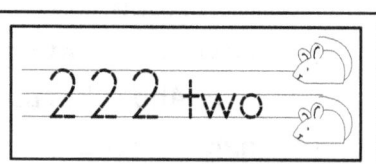

Learning About Letters Book

Have children color, cut out, and glue shapes on shapes pages (p. 64). Form a book with each child's complete set of alphabet or number shape pages. Cut construction paper covers for children to decorate. Write "Learning About Letters" or "Learning About Numbers" on the covers. Staple each child's cover and set of shape pages in order.

Scribble Scribble Picture Books

Provide children with crayons to color and fill in the missing letter or numeral on each picture book page. Have children cut out picture book pages to form an Alphabet or Counting Picture Book. Punch two holes along the left margin of each page. Cut, lace, and tie a length of yarn through the holes to bind the pages in order.

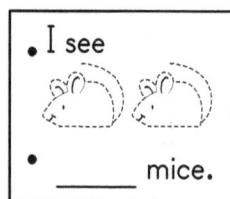

Connect-the-Letters, Connect-the-Numbers

Reproduce connect-the-dot activity pages for children to practice letter and number sequencing. Provide children with crayons to connect-the-dots and color the pages. The option at the bottom of each connect-the-dot page explains how to make hanging pictures from connect-the-dot activity pages. Children can also glue on pom poms, cereal Os, and more to make creative textured works of art.

Scribble Scribble Finger Puppets and Props

Reproduce, color, laminate, and cut out alphabet picture shapes. Tape a paper ring band to the back of each shape to form a finger puppet or prop. Children can wear the puppets and props during an "I Know My ABCs" sing-along.

Learning About Letter Aa

Trace the letters. Color, cut out, and glue the letter strip on a Writing Practice Page (page 64).

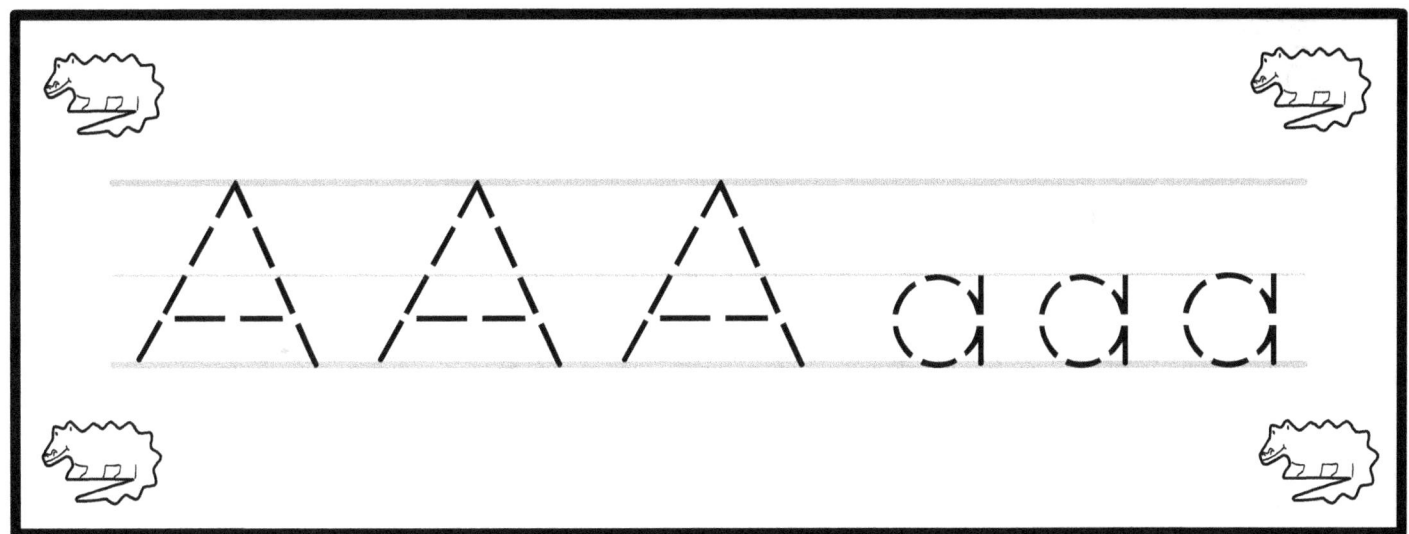

Letter Aa Picture Shapes

Color the pictures.
Cut out the shapes.
Glue each shape on
a Shapes Page (page 64).
Add the page to a
Learning About
Letters Book.

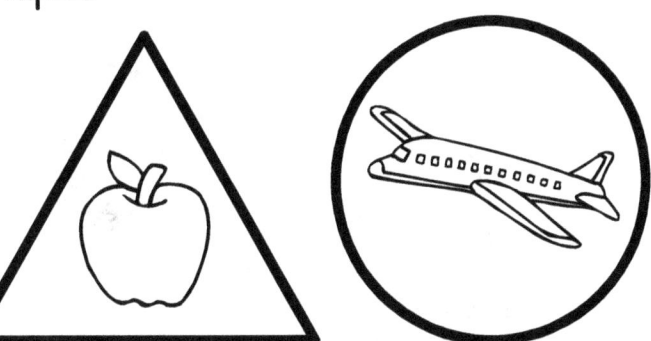 

Alphabet Picture Book Page

Trace the picture.
Color the picture.
Fill in the missing letter.
Cut out the picture.
Punch a hole at each dot.
Add the page to an
Alphabet Picture Book.

I see an ___lligator.

Learning About Letter Bb

Trace the letters. Color, cut out, and glue the letter strip on a Writing Practice Page (page 64).

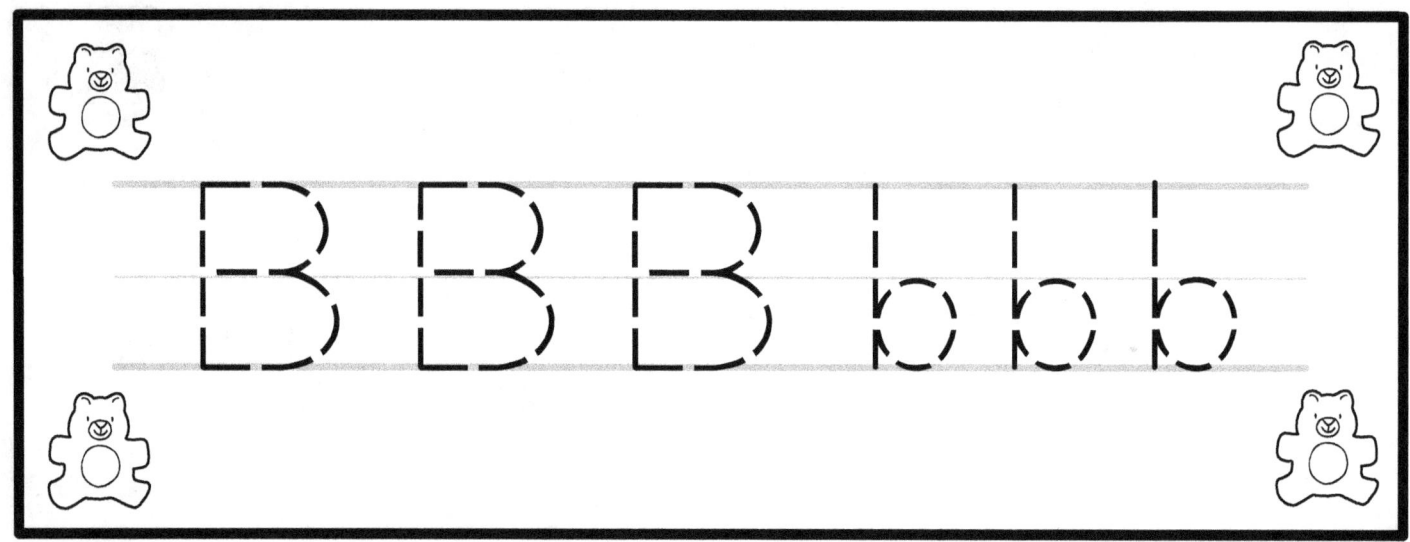

Letter Bb Picture Shapes

Color the pictures.
Cut out the shapes.
Glue each shape on
a Shapes Page (page 64).
Add the page to a
Learning About
Letters Book.

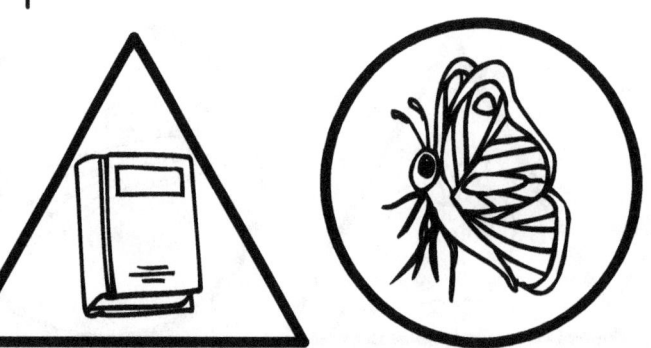 

Alphabet Picture Book Page

Trace the picture.
Color the picture.
Fill in the missing letter.
Cut out the picture.
Punch a hole at each dot.
Add the page to an
Alphabet Picture Book.

Learning About Letter Cc

Trace the letters. Color, cut out, and glue the letter strip on a Writing Practice Page (page 64).

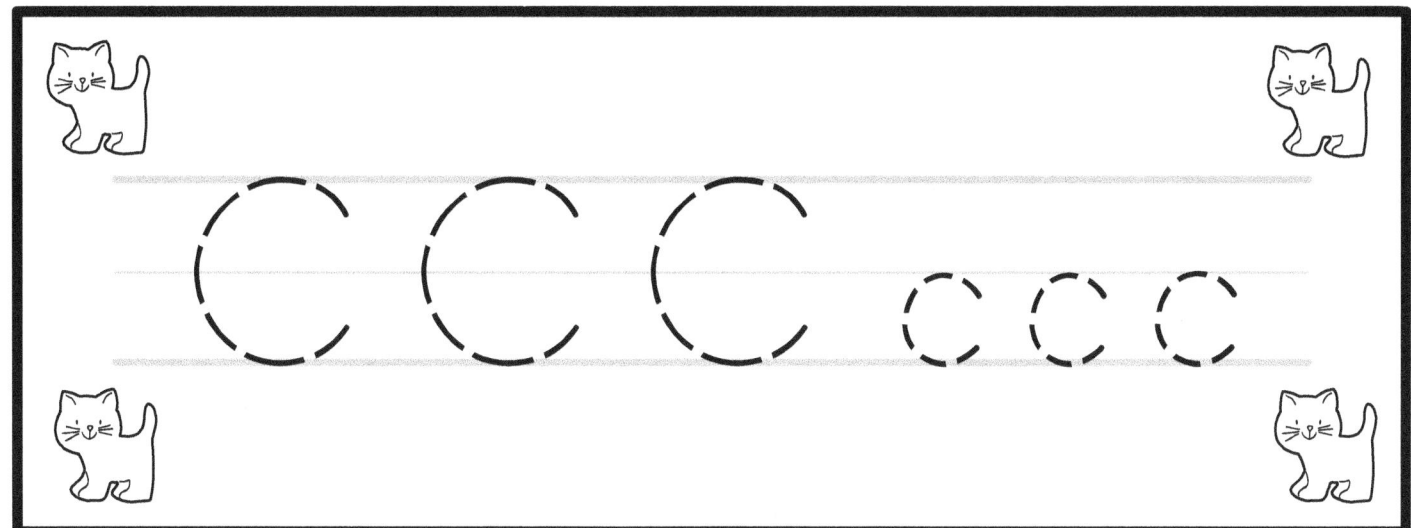

Letter Cc Picture Shapes

Color the pictures.
Cut out the shapes.
Glue each shape on
a Shapes Page (page 64).
Add the page to a
Learning About
Letters Book.

Alphabet Picture Book Page

Trace the picture.
Color the picture.
Fill in the missing letter.
Cut out the picture.
Punch a hole at each dot.
Add the page to an
Alphabet Picture Book.

I see

a ___ at.

Learning About Letter Dd

Trace the letters. Color, cut out, and glue the letter strip on a Writing Practice Page (page 64).

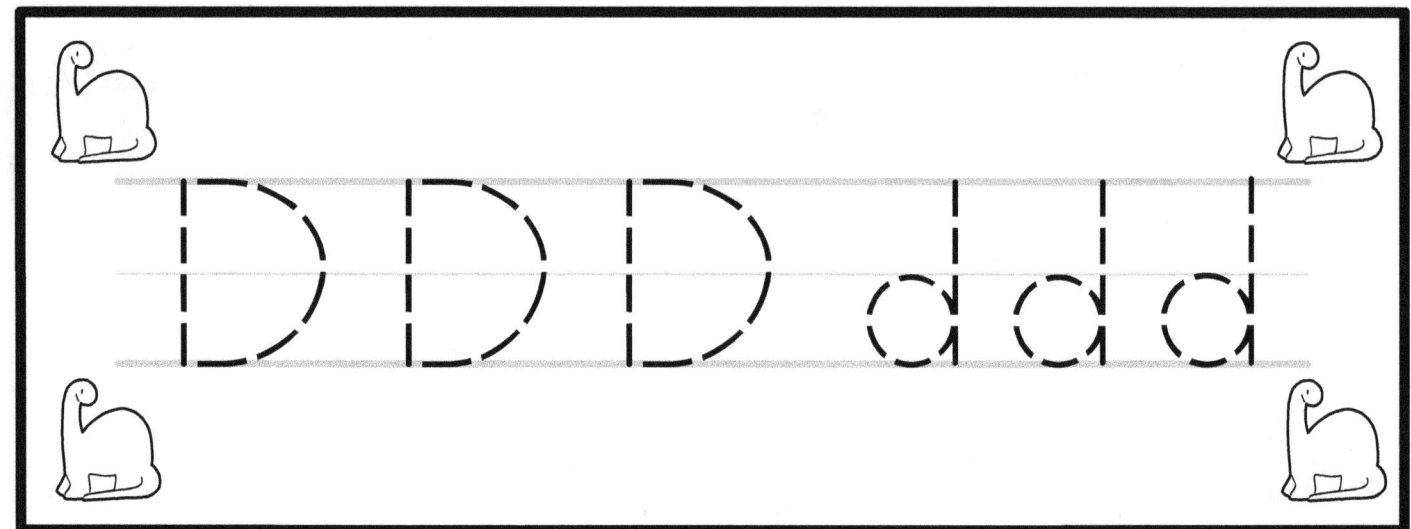

Letter Dd Picture Shapes

Color the pictures.
Cut out the shapes.
Glue each shape on
a Shapes Page (page 64).
Add the page to a
Learning About
Letters Book.

Alphabet Picture Book Page

Trace the picture.
Color the picture.
Fill in the missing letter.
Cut out the picture.
Punch a hole at each dot.
Add the page to an
Alphabet Picture Book.

I see a ___inosaur.

Learning About Letter Ee

Trace the letters. Color, cut out, and glue the letter strip on a Writing Practice Page (page 64).

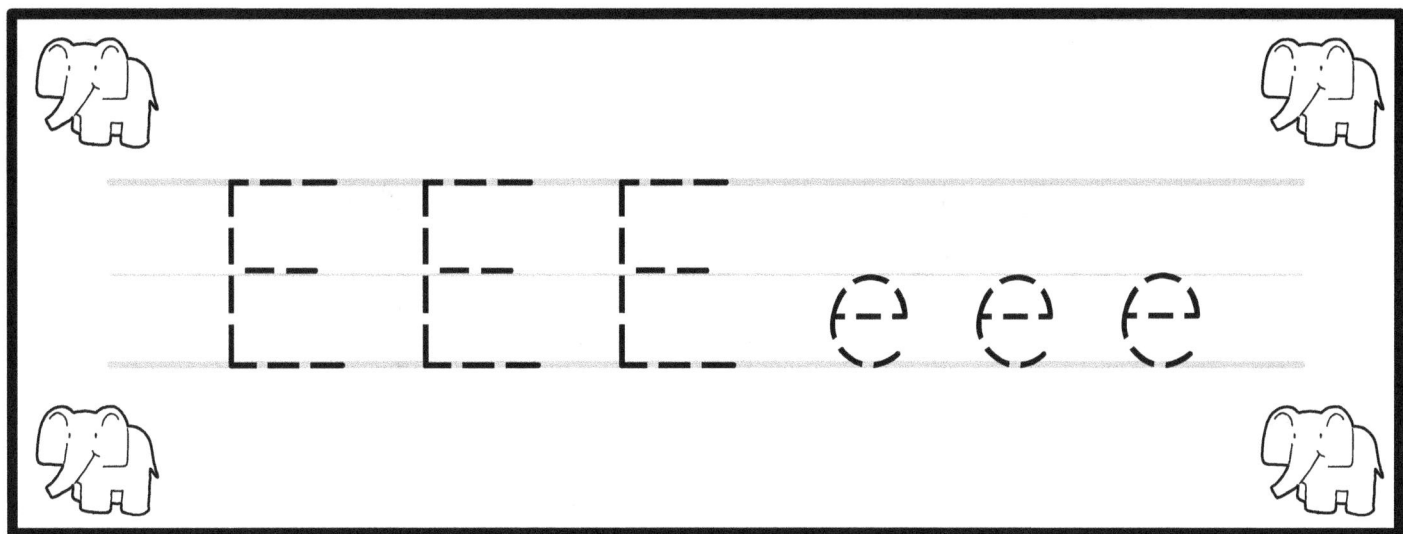

Letter Ee Picture Shapes

Color the pictures.
Cut out the shapes.
Glue each shape on
a Shapes Page (page 64).
Add the page to a
Learning About
Letters Book.

Alphabet Picture Book Page

Trace the picture.
Color the picture.
Fill in the missing letter.
Cut out the picture.
Punch a hole at each dot.
Add the page to an
Alphabet Picture Book.

Learning About Letter Ff

Trace the letters. Color, cut out, and glue the letter strip on a Writing Practice Page (page 64).

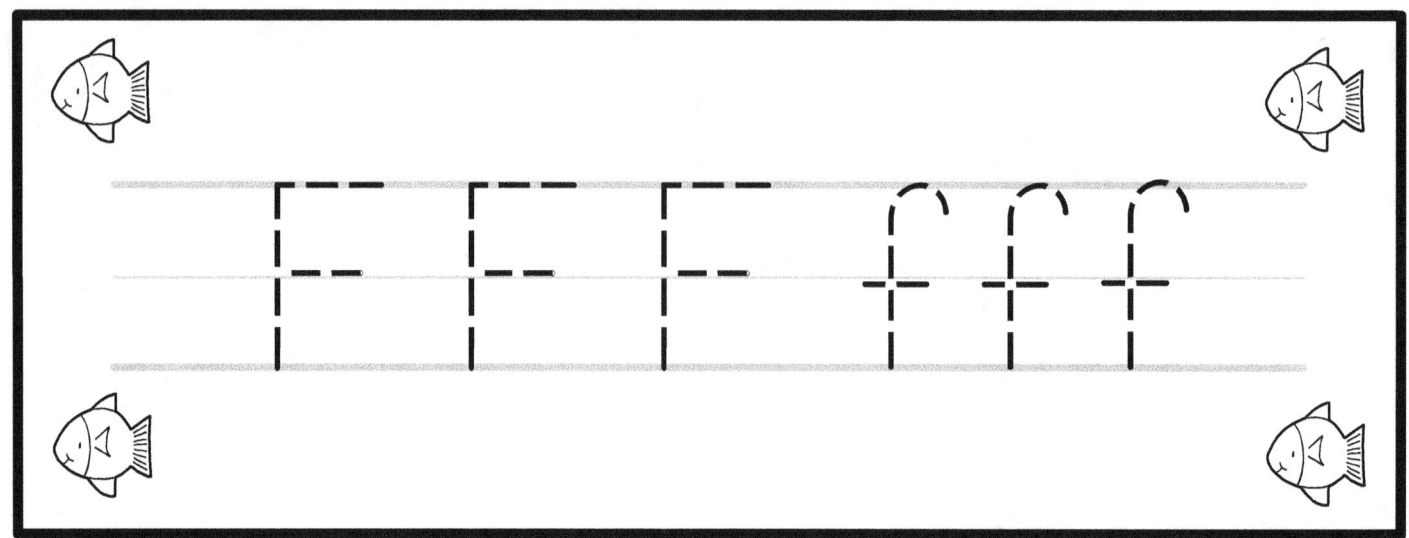

Letter Ff Picture Shapes
Color the pictures.
Cut out the shapes.
Glue each shape on
a Shapes Page (page 64).
Add the page to a
Learning About
Letters Book.

Alphabet Picture Book Page
Trace the picture.
Color the picture.
Fill in the missing letter.
Cut out the picture.
Punch a hole at each dot.
Add the page to an
Alphabet Picture Book.

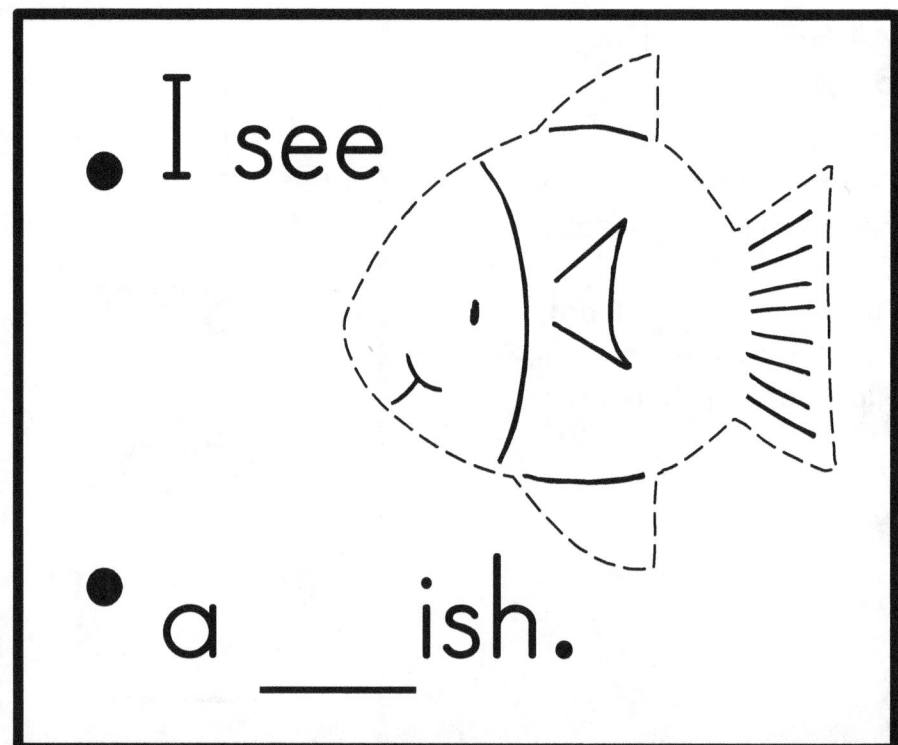

Learning About Letter Gg

Trace the letters. Color, cut out, and glue the letter strip on a Writing Practice Page (page 64).

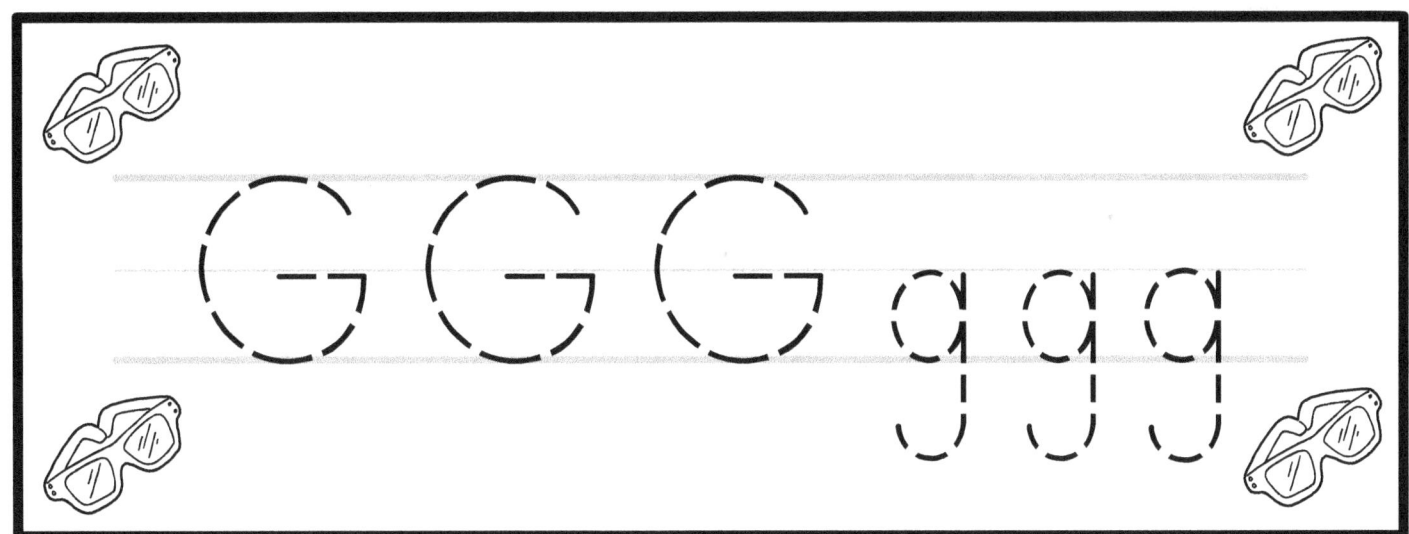

Letter Gg Picture Shapes
Color the pictures.
Cut out the shapes.
Glue each shape on
a Shapes Page (page 64).
Add the page to a
Learning About
Letters Book.

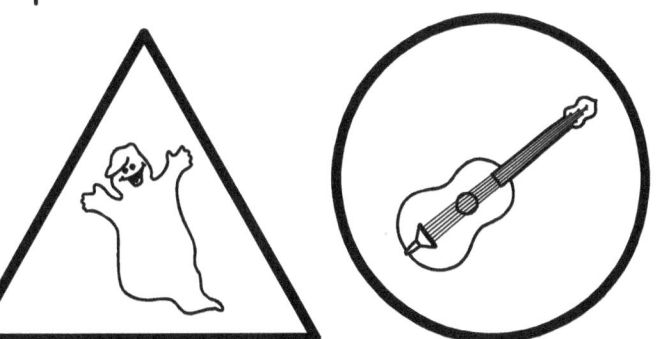 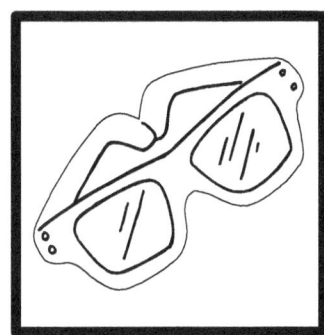

Alphabet Picture Book Page
Trace the picture.
Color the picture.
Fill in the missing letter.
Cut out the picture.
Punch a hole at each dot.
Add the page to an
Alphabet Picture Book.

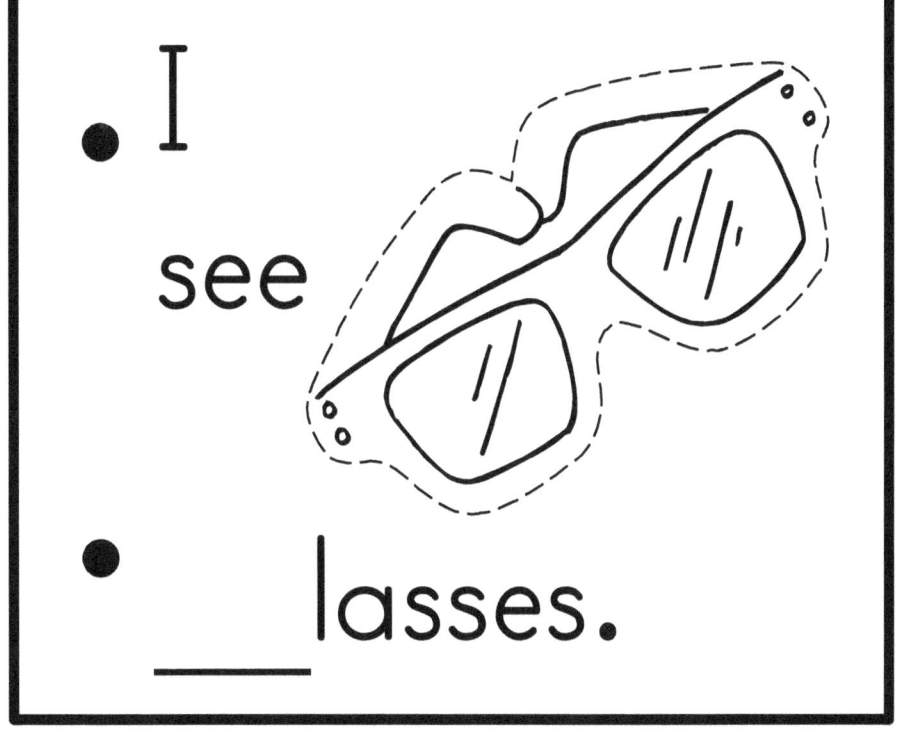

I see ___lasses.

LAB20132 • SCRIBBLE SCRIBBLE • 978-1-937257-19-4   11   ©2013 Little Acorn Books™

Learning About Letter Hh

Trace the letters. Color, cut out, and glue the letter strip on a Writing Practice Page (page 64).

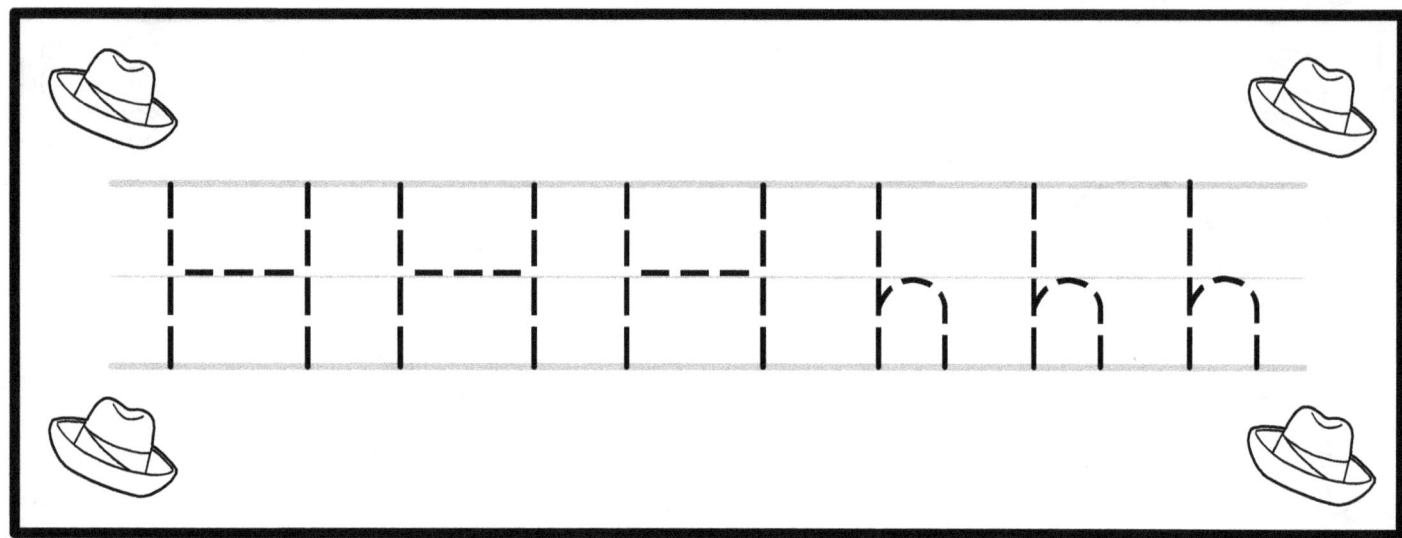

Letter Hh Picture Shapes

Color the pictures.
Cut out the shapes.
Glue each shape on
a Shapes Page (page 64).
Add the page to a
Learning About
Letters Book.

Alphabet Picture Book Page

Trace the picture.
Color the picture.
Fill in the missing letter.
Cut out the picture.
Punch a hole at each dot.
Add the page to an
Alphabet Picture Book.

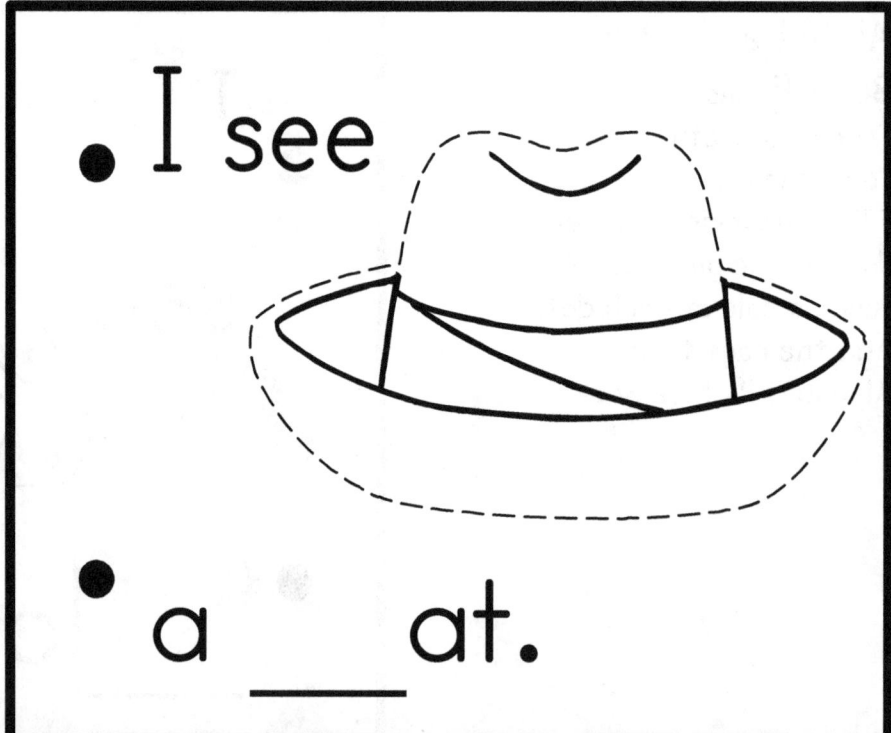

I see a ___at.

Learning About Letter Ii

Trace the letters. Color, cut out, and glue the letter strip on a Writing Practice Page (page 64).

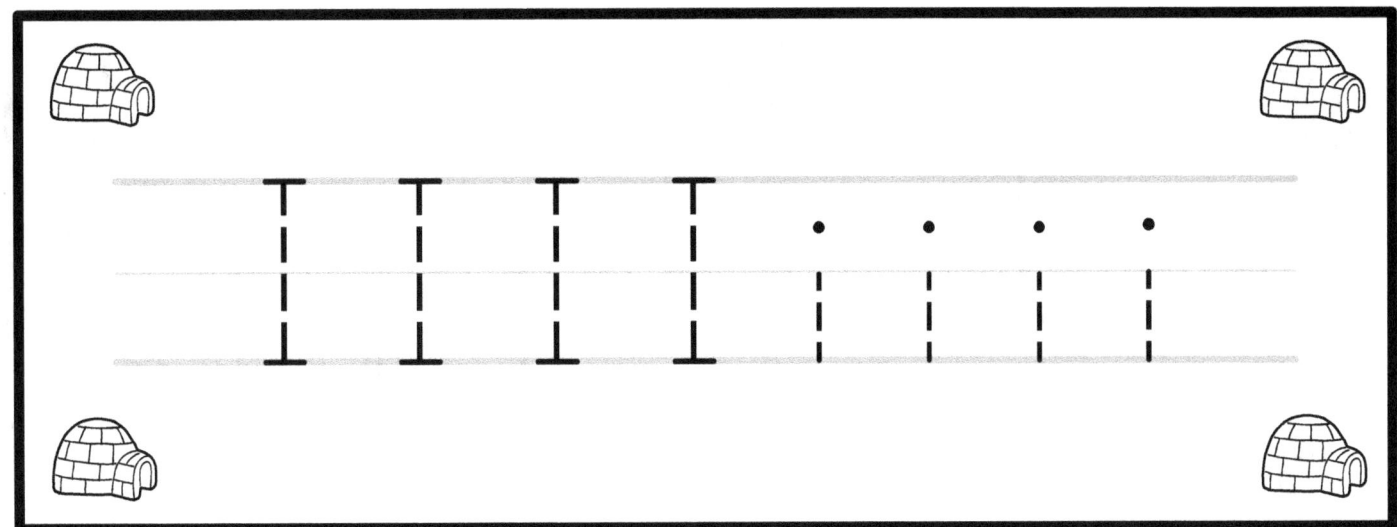

Letter Ii Picture Shapes

Color the pictures.
Cut out the shapes.
Glue each shape on
a Shapes Page (page 64).
Add the page to a
Learning About
Letters Book.

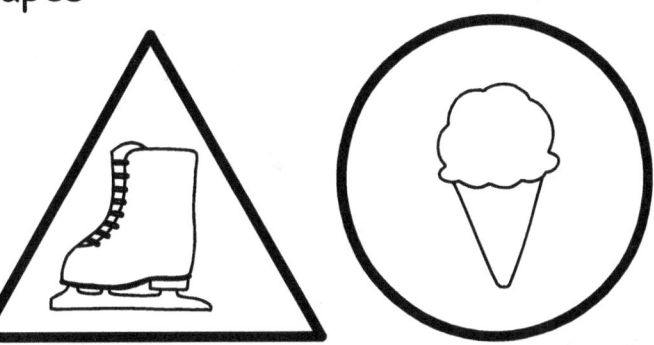

Alphabet Picture Book Page

Trace the picture.
Color the picture.
Fill in the missing letter.
Cut out the picture.
Punch a hole at each dot.
Add the page to an
Alphabet Picture Book.

Learning About Letter Jj

Trace the letters. Color, cut out, and glue the letter strip on a Writing Practice Page (page 64).

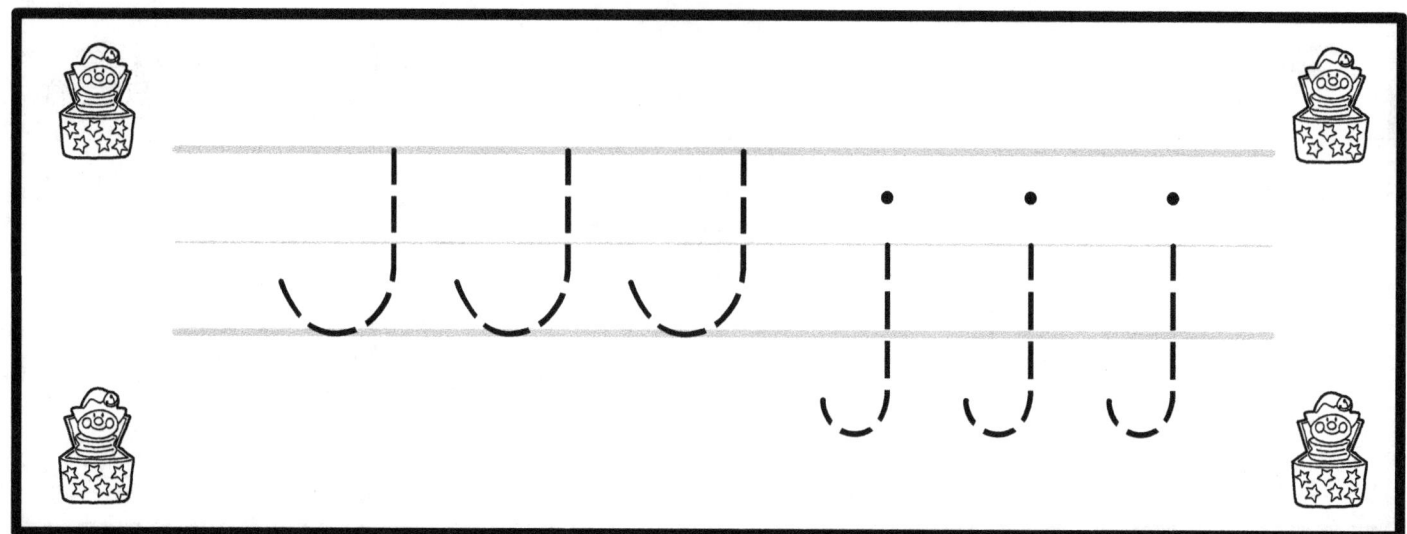

Letter Jj Picture Shapes
Color the pictures.
Cut out the shapes.
Glue each shape on
a Shapes Page (page 64).
Add the page to a
Learning About
Letters Book.

Alphabet Picture Book Page
Trace the picture.
Color the picture.
Fill in the missing letter.
Cut out the picture.
Punch a hole at each dot.
Add the page to an
Alphabet Picture Book.

I see a ___ack-in-the-box.

Learning About Letter Kk

Trace the letters. Color, cut out, and glue the letter strip on a Writing Practice Page (page 64).

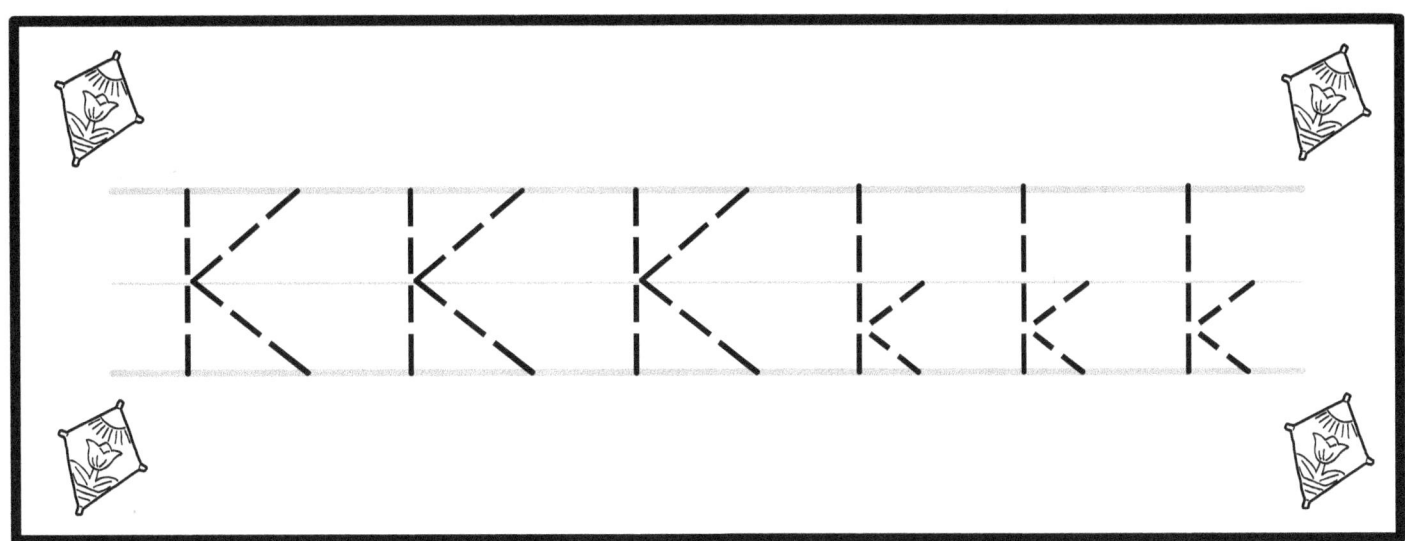

Letter Kk Picture Shapes

Color the pictures.
Cut out the shapes.
Glue each shape on
a Shapes Page (page 64).
Add the page to a
Learning About
Letters Book.

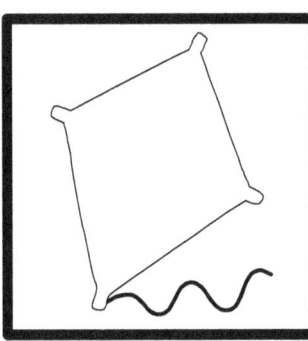

Alphabet Picture Book Page

Trace the picture.
Color the picture.
Fill in the missing letter.
Cut out the picture.
Punch a hole at each dot.
Add the page to an
Alphabet Picture Book.

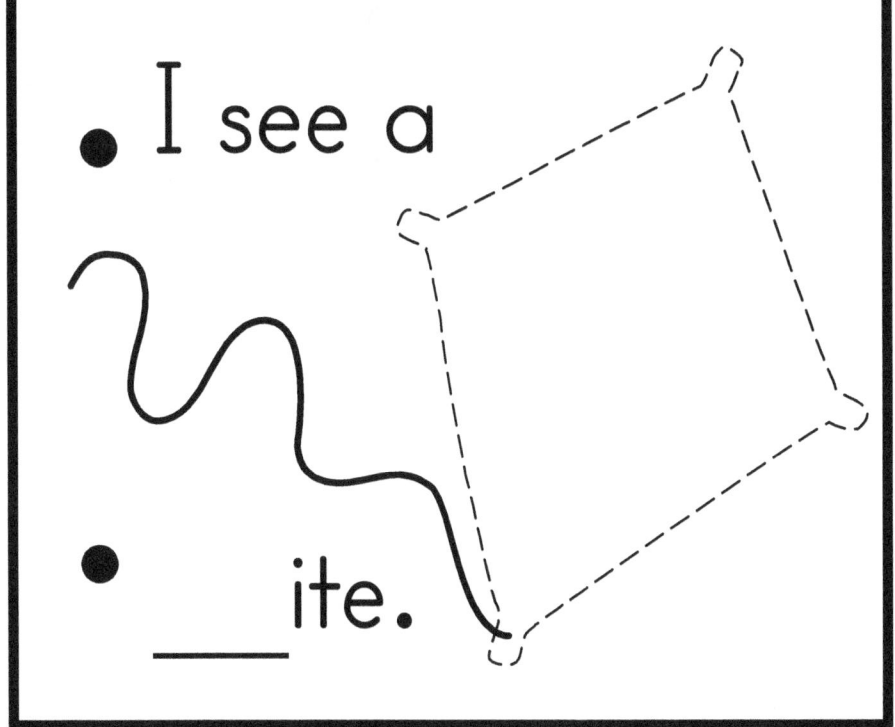

I see a ___ite.

Learning About Letter Ll

Trace the letters. Color, cut out, and glue the letter strip on a Writing Practice Page (page 64).

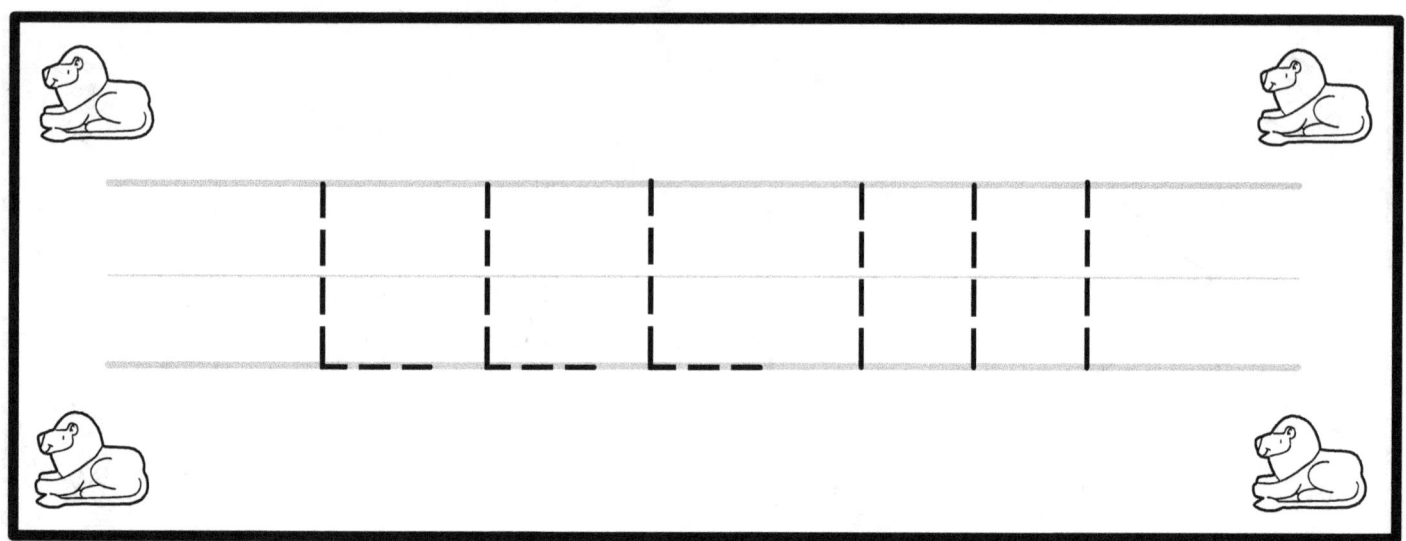

Letter Ll Picture Shapes

Color the pictures.
Cut out the shapes.
Glue each shape on
a Shapes Page (page 64).
Add the page to a
Learning About
Letters Book.

Alphabet Picture Book Page

Trace the picture.
Color the picture.
Fill in the missing letter.
Cut out the picture.
Punch a hole at each dot.
Add the page to an
Alphabet Picture Book.

LAB20132 • SCRIBBLE SCRIBBLE • 978-1-937257-19-4   16   ©2013 Little Acorn Books™

Learning About Letter Mm

Trace the letters. Color, cut out, and glue the letter strip on a Writing Practice Page (page 64).

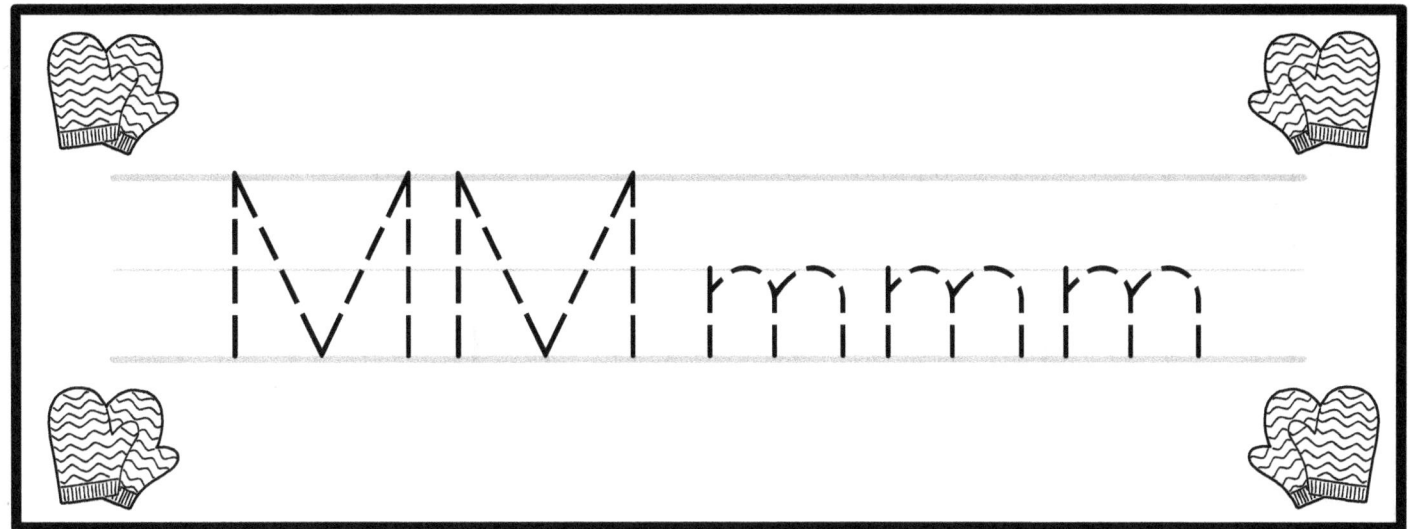

Letter Mm Picture Shapes
Color the pictures.
Cut out the shapes.
Glue each shape on
a Shapes Page (page 64).
Add the page to a
Learning About
Letters Book.

  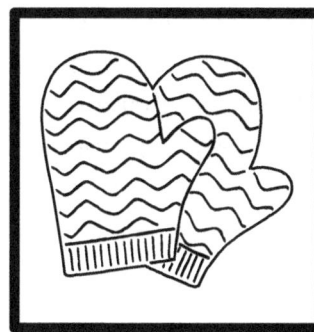

Alphabet Picture Book Page
Trace the picture.
Color the picture.
Fill in the missing letter.
Cut out the picture.
Punch a hole at each dot.
Add the page to an
Alphabet Picture Book.

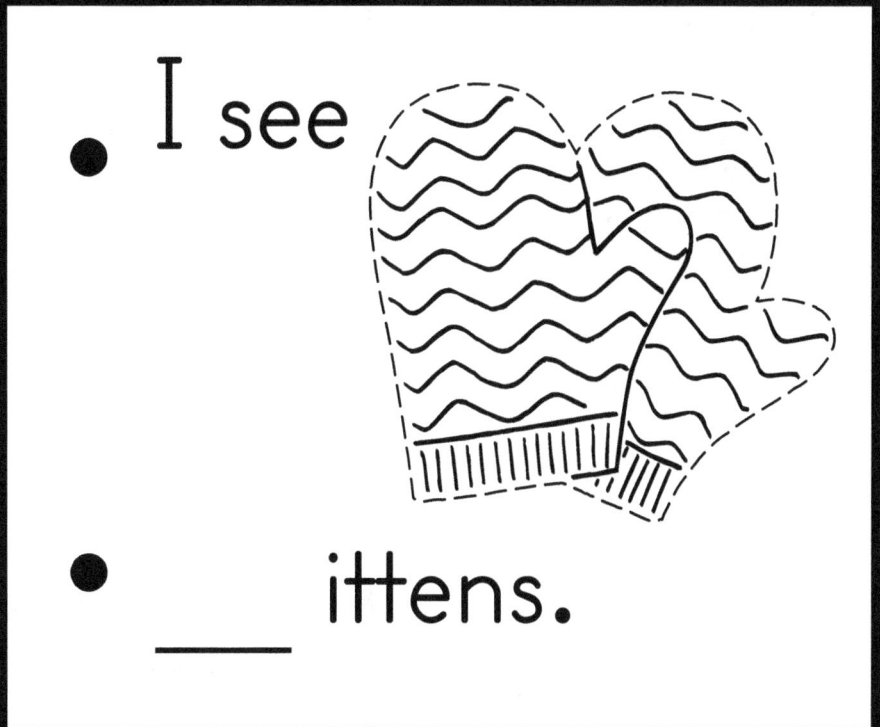

I see

___ ittens.

Learning About Letter Nn

Trace the letters. Color, cut out, and glue the letter strip on a Writing Practice Page (page 64).

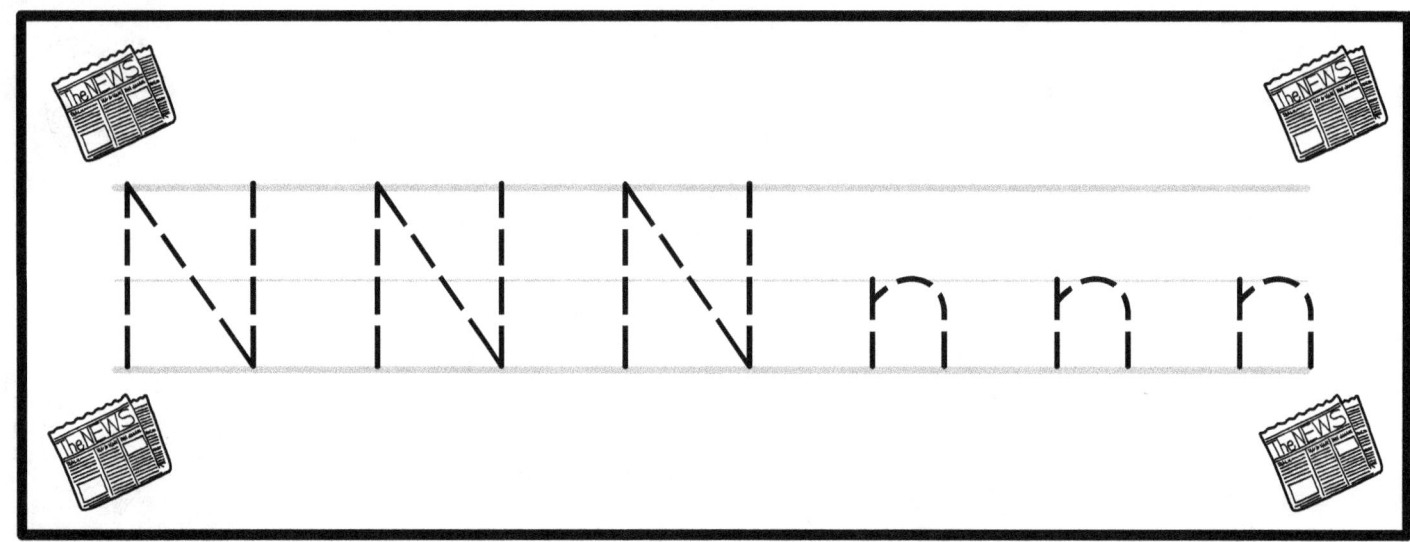

Letter Nn Picture Shapes

Color the pictures.
Cut out the shapes.
Glue each shape on
a Shapes Page (page 64).
Add the page to a
Learning About
Letters Book.

Alphabet Picture Book Page

Trace the picture.
Color the picture.
Fill in the missing letter.
Cut out the picture.
Punch a hole at each dot.
Add the page to an
Alphabet Picture Book.

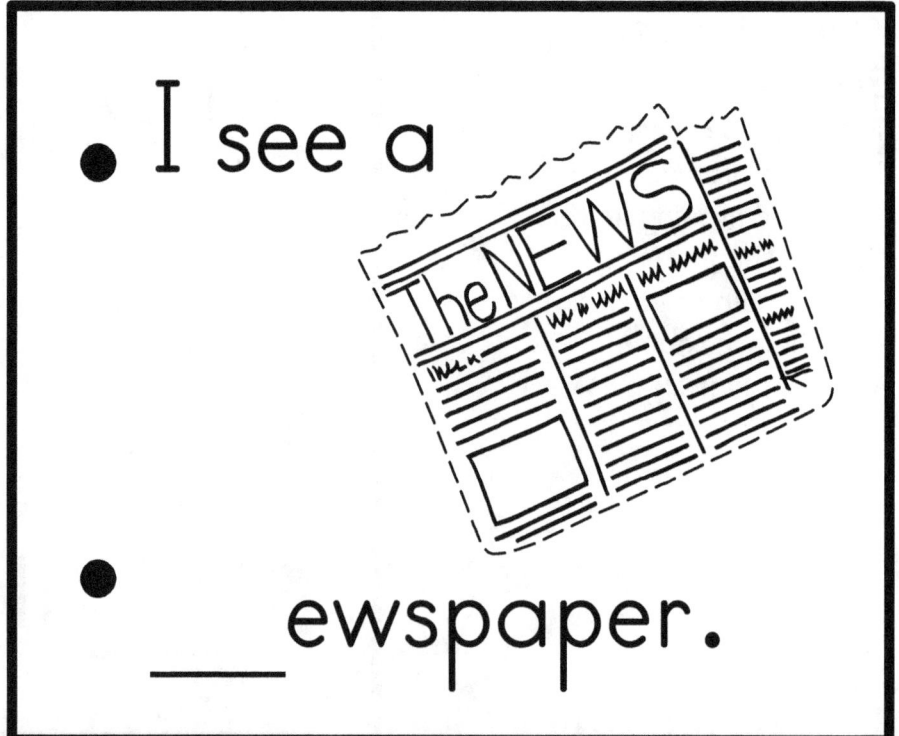

• I see a

• ___ewspaper.

Learning About Letter Oo

Trace the letters. Color, cut out, and glue the letter strip on a Writing Practice Page (page 64).

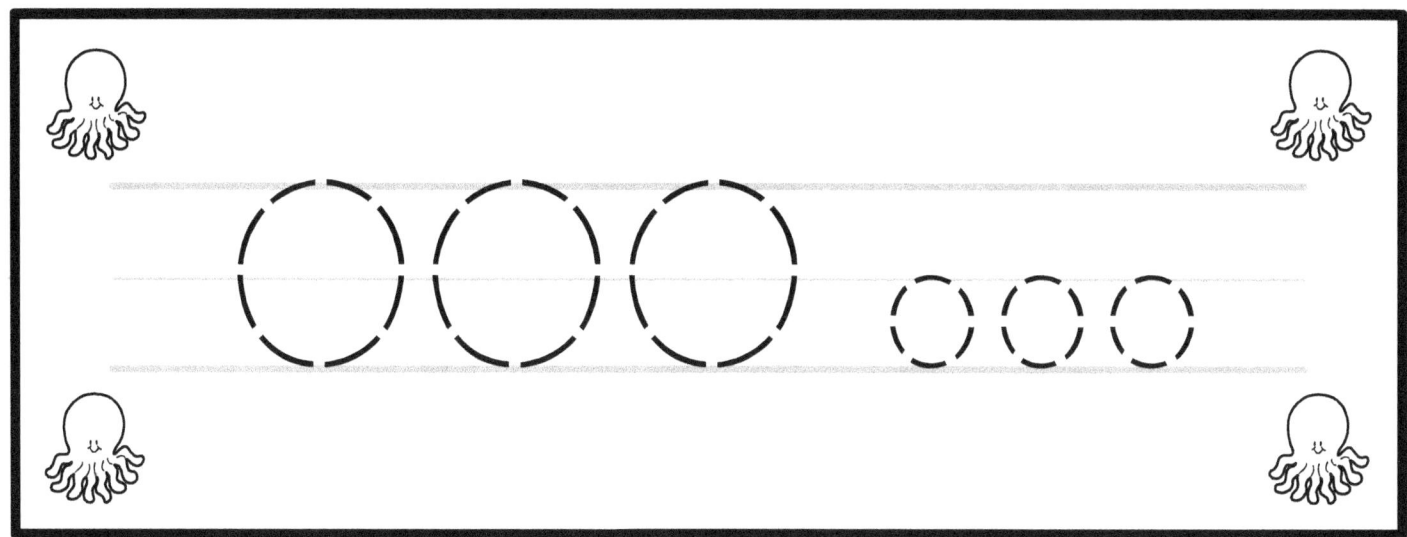

Letter Oo Picture Shapes

Color the pictures.
Cut out the shapes.
Glue each shape on
a Shapes Page (page 64).
Add the page to a
Learning About
Letters Book.

Alphabet Picture Book Page

Trace the picture.
Color the picture.
Fill in the missing letter.
Cut out the picture.
Punch a hole at each dot.
Add the page to an
Alphabet Picture Book.

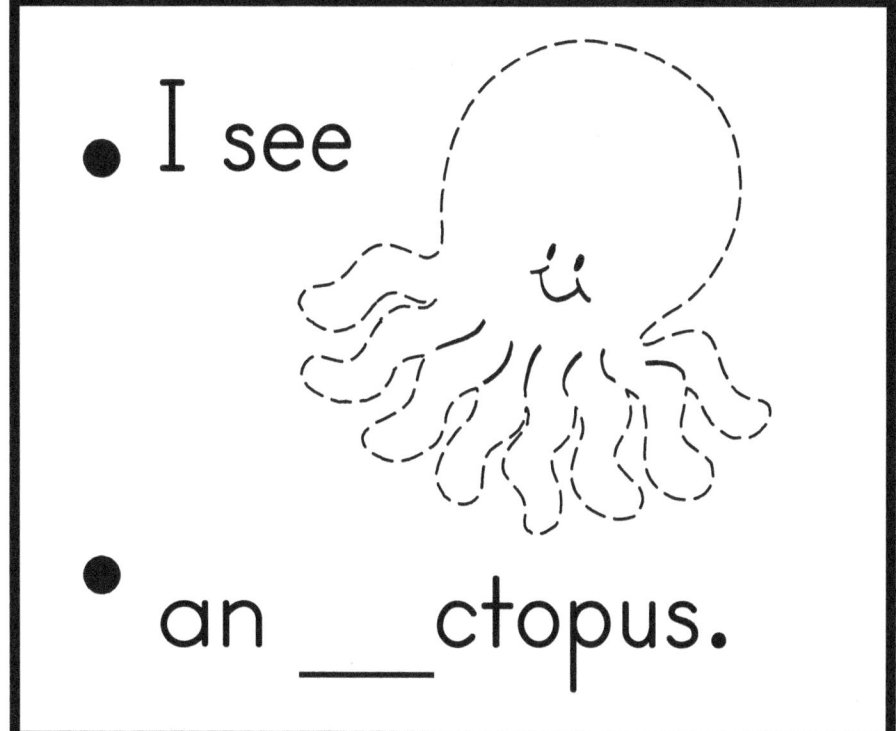

Learning About Letter Pp

Trace the letters. Color, cut out, and glue the letter strip on a Writing Practice Page (page 64).

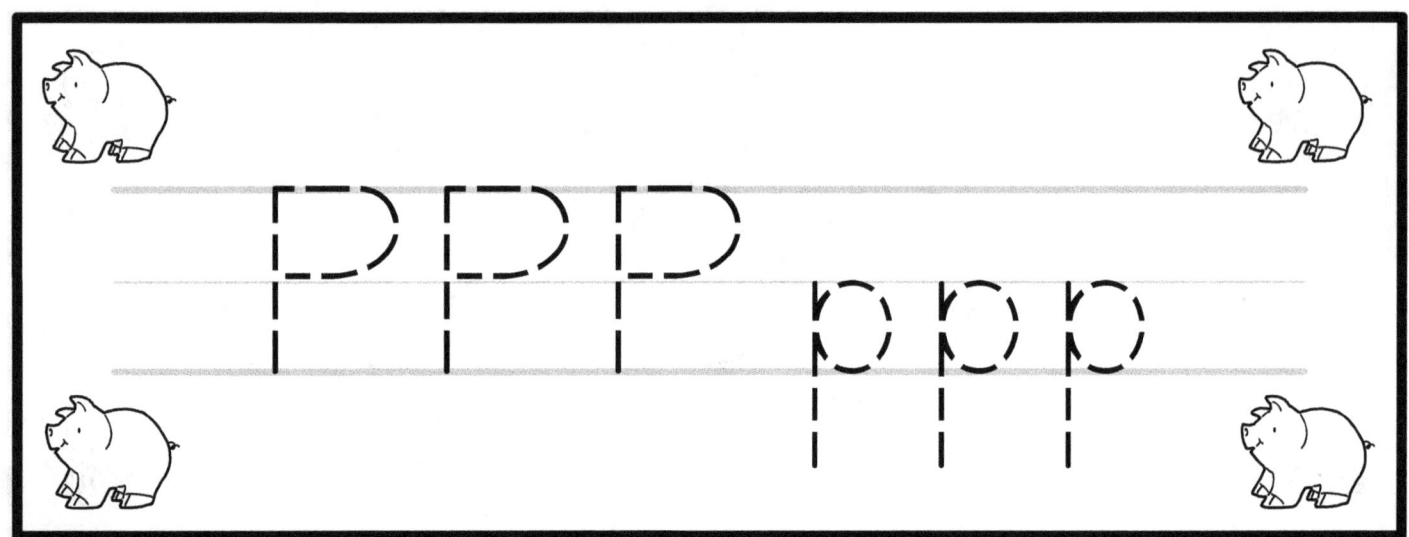

Letter Pp Picture Shapes
Color the pictures.
Cut out the shapes.
Glue each shape on
a Shapes Page (page 64).
Add the page to a
Learning About
Letters Book.

**Alphabet Picture
Book Page**
Trace the picture.
Color the picture.
Fill in the missing letter.
Cut out the picture.
Punch a hole at each dot.
Add the page to an
Alphabet Picture Book.

Learning About Letter Qq

Trace the letters. Color, cut out, and glue the letter strip on a Writing Practice Page (page 64).

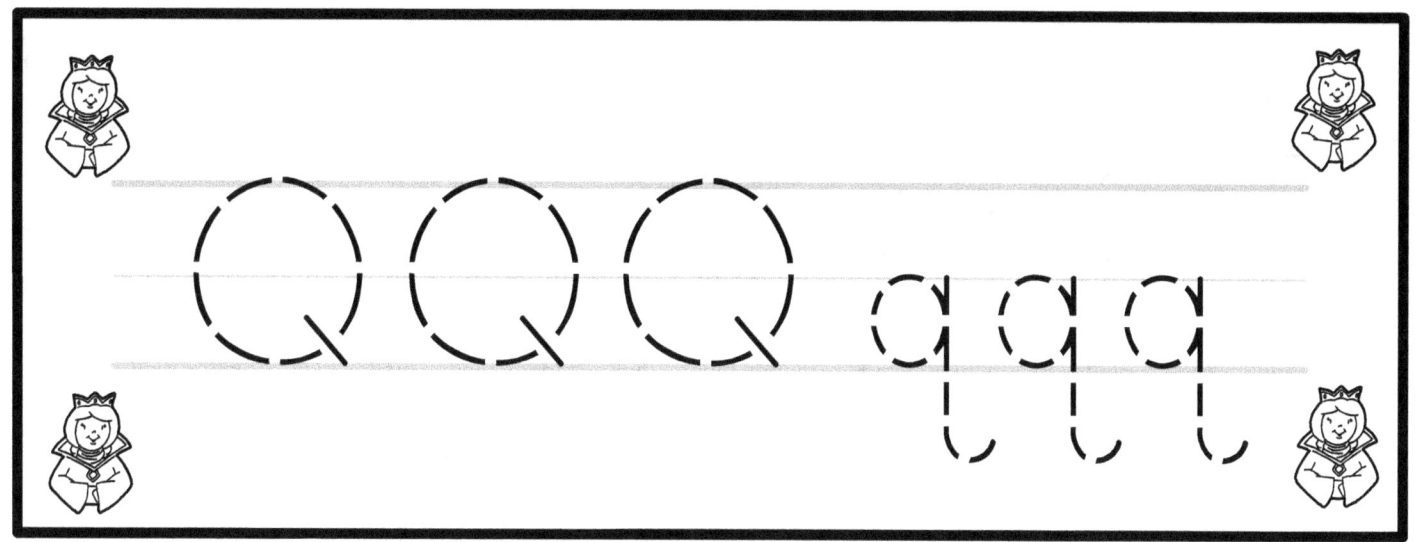

Letter Qq Picture Shapes

Color the pictures.
Cut out the shapes.
Glue each shape on
a Shapes Page (page 64).
Add the page to a
Learning About
Letters Book.

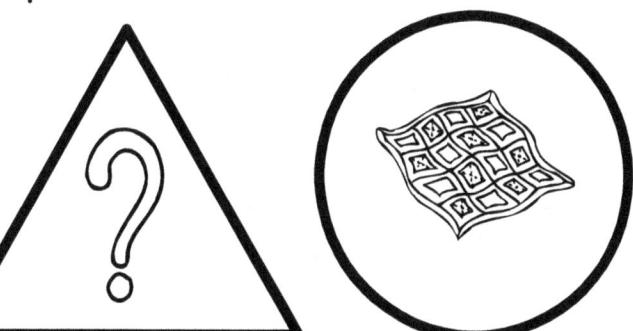

Alphabet Picture Book Page

Trace the picture.
Color the picture.
Fill in the missing letter.
Cut out the picture.
Punch a hole at each dot.
Add the page to an
Alphabet Picture Book.

• I see a

• ___ueen.

Learning About Letter Rr

Trace the letters. Color, cut out, and glue the letter strip on a Writing Practice Page (page 64).

Letter Rr Picture Shapes

Color the pictures.
Cut out the shapes.
Glue each shape on
a Shapes Page (page 64).
Add the page to a
Learning About
Letters Book.

Alphabet Picture Book Page

Trace the picture.
Color the picture.
Fill in the missing letter.
Cut out the picture.
Punch a hole at each dot.
Add the page to an
Alphabet Picture Book.

I see a

___abbit.

Learning About Letter Ss

Trace the letters. Color, cut out, and glue the letter strip on a Writing Practice Page (page 64).

Letter Ss Picture Shapes
Color the pictures.
Cut out the shapes.
Glue each shape on
a Shapes Page (page 64).
Add the page to a
Learning About
Letters Book.

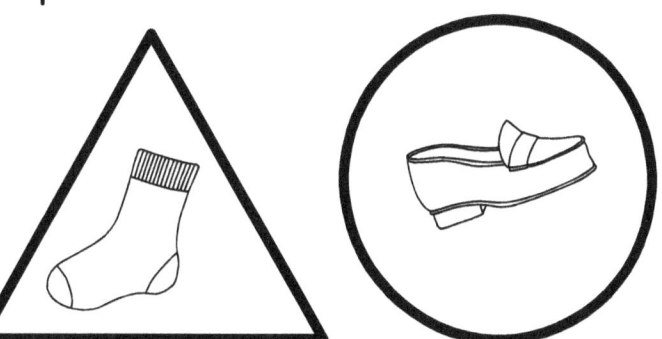

Alphabet Picture Book Page
Trace the picture.
Color the picture.
Fill in the missing letter.
Cut out the picture.
Punch a hole at each dot.
Add the page to an
Alphabet Picture Book.

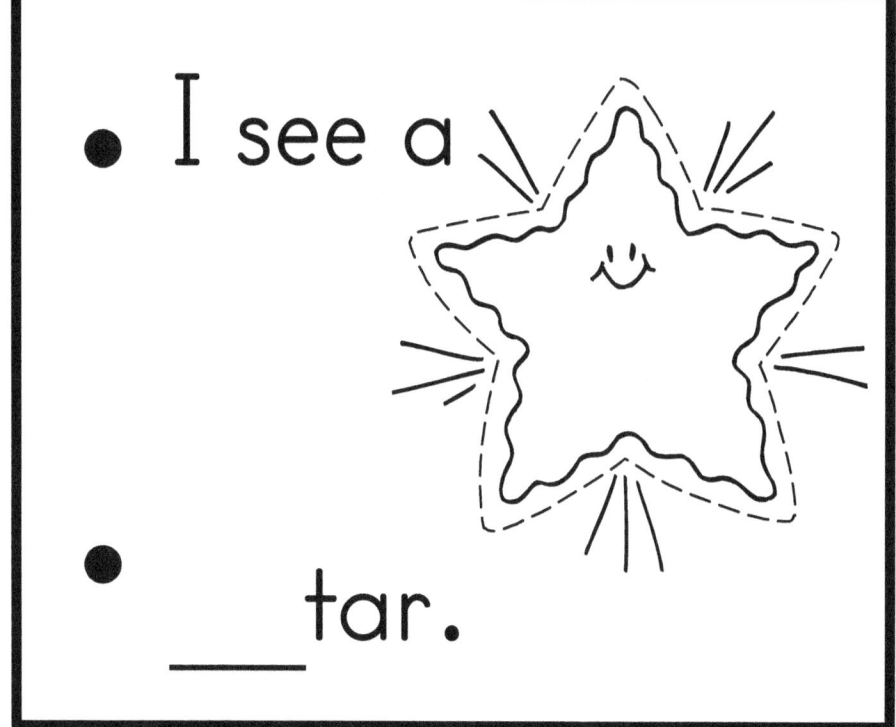

I see a

___tar.

Learning About Letter Tt

Trace the letters. Color, cut out, and glue the letter strip on a Writing Practice Page (page 64).

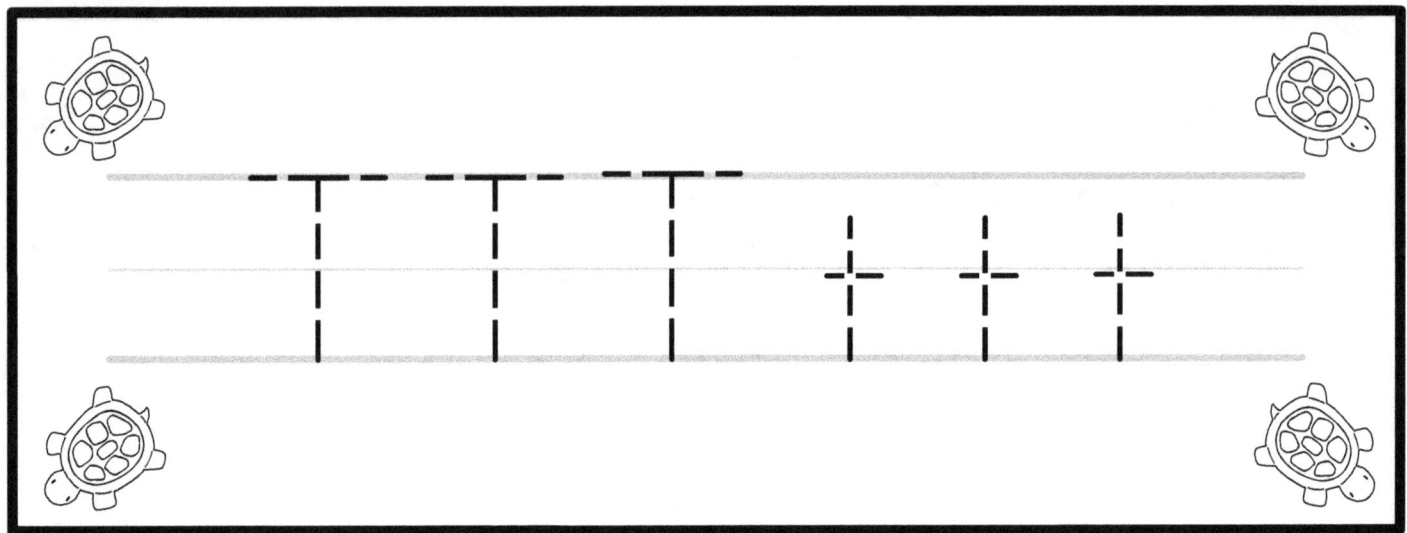

Letter Tt Picture Shapes
Color the pictures.
Cut out the shapes.
Glue each shape on
a Shapes Page (page 64).
Add the page to a
Learning About
Letters Book.

Alphabet Picture Book Page
Trace the picture.
Color the picture.
Fill in the missing letter.
Cut out the picture.
Punch a hole at each dot.
Add the page to an
Alphabet Picture Book.

• I see

• a ___urtle.

Learning About Letter Uu

Trace the letters. Color, cut out, and glue the letter strip on a Writing Practice Page (page 64).

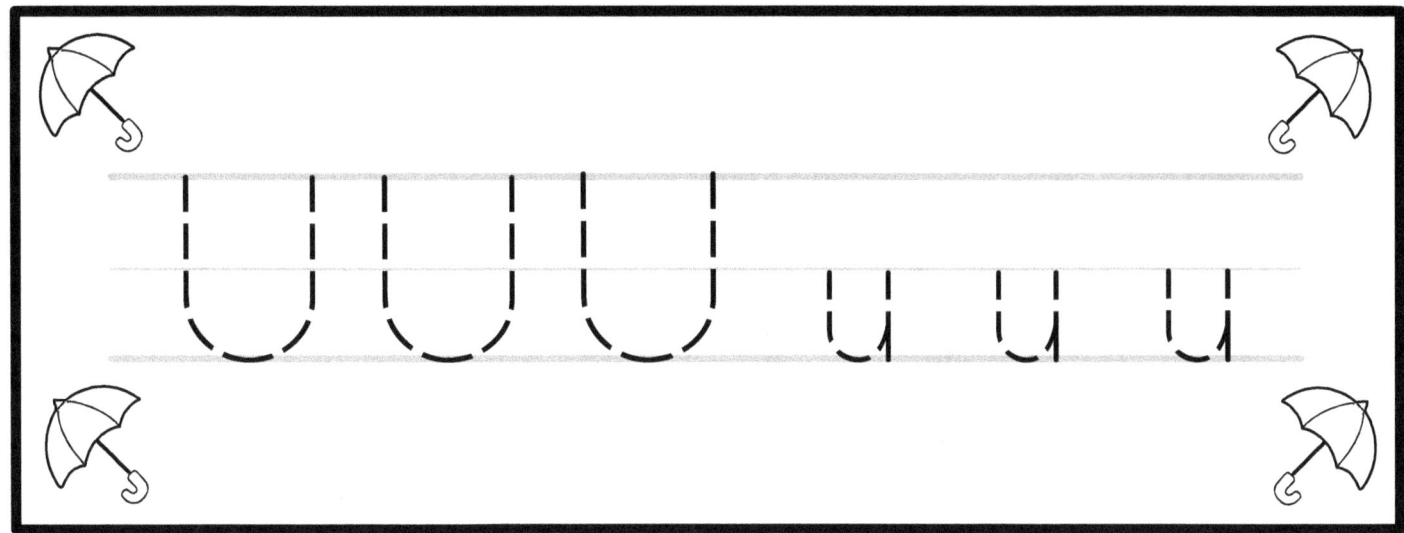

Letter Uu Picture Shapes
Color the pictures.
Cut out the shapes.
Glue each shape on
a Shapes Page (page 64).
Add the page to a
Learning About
Letters Book.

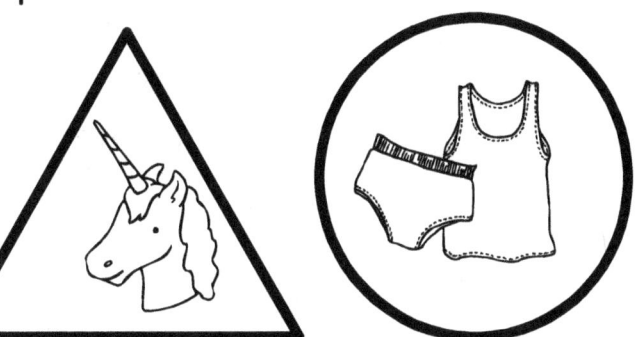 

Alphabet Picture Book Page
Trace the picture.
Color the picture.
Fill in the missing letter.
Cut out the picture.
Punch a hole at each dot.
Add the page to an
Alphabet Picture Book.

• I see an

• ___mbrella.

Learning About Letter Vv

Trace the letters. Color, cut out, and glue the letter strip on a Writing Practice Page (page 64).

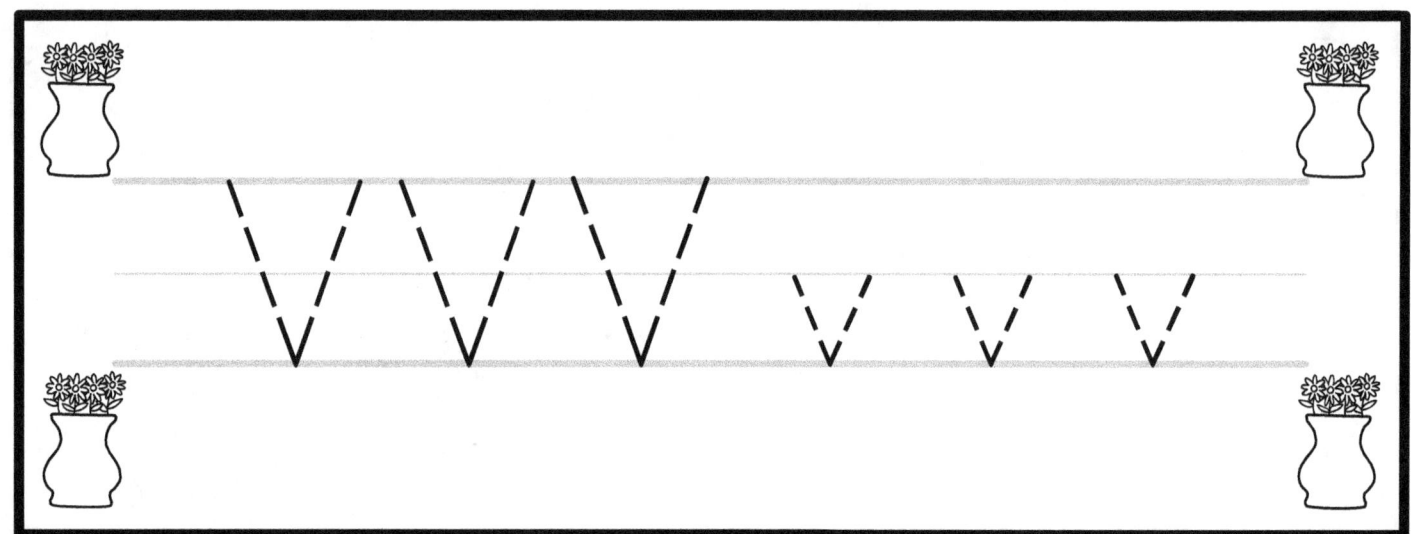

Letter Vv Picture Shapes
Color the pictures.
Cut out the shapes.
Glue each shape on
a Shapes Page (page 64).
Add the page to a
Learning About
Letters Book.

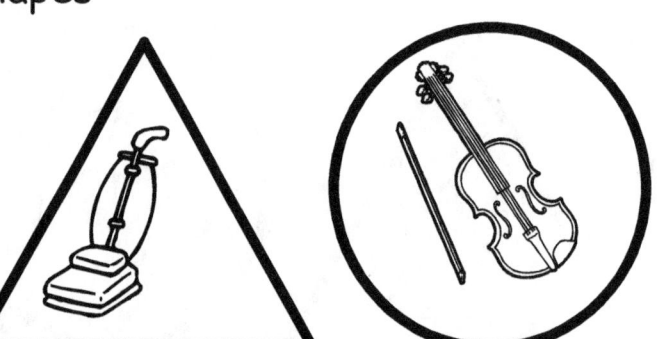 

Alphabet Picture Book Page
Trace the picture.
Color the picture.
Fill in the missing letter.
Cut out the picture.
Punch a hole at each dot.
Add the page to an
Alphabet Picture Book.

• I see a

• ___ase.

Learning About Letter Ww

Trace the letters. Color, cut out, and glue the letter strip on a Writing Practice Page (page 64).

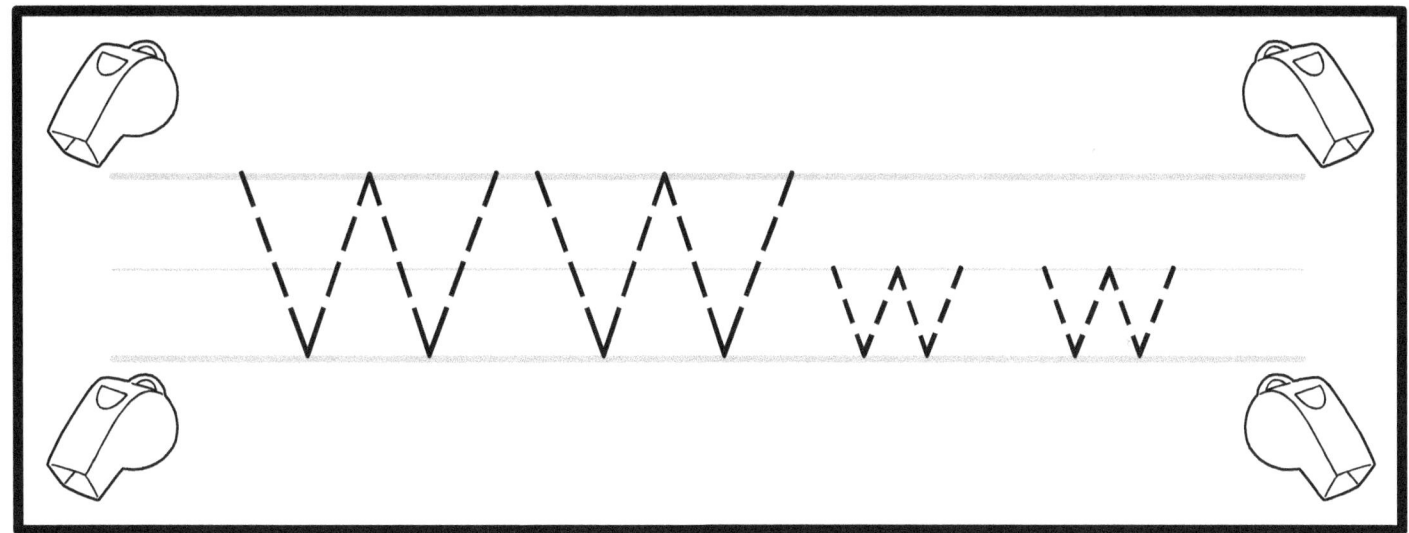

Letter Ww Picture Shapes

Color the pictures.
Cut out the shapes.
Glue each shape on a Shapes Page (page 64).
Add the page to a Learning About Letters Book.

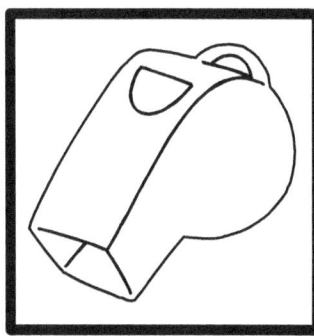

Alphabet Picture Book Page

Trace the picture.
Color the picture.
Fill in the missing letter.
Cut out the picture.
Punch a hole at each dot.
Add the page to an Alphabet Picture Book.

Learning About Letter Xx

Trace the letters. Color, cut out, and glue the letter strip on a Writing Practice Page (page 64).

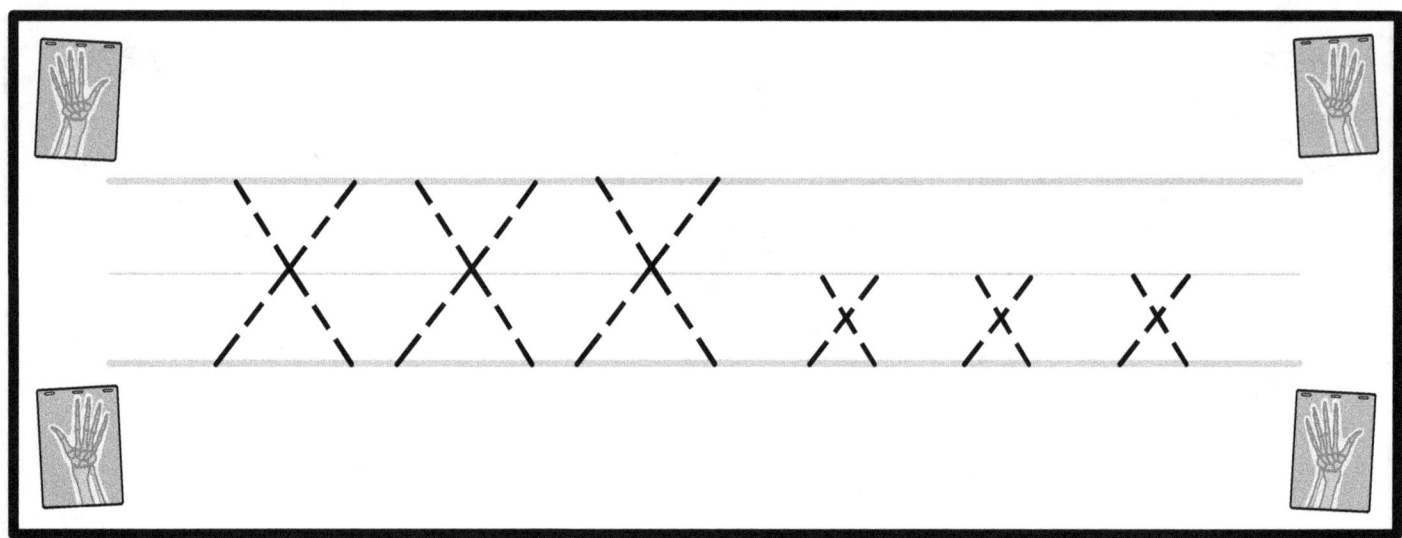

Letter Xx Picture Shapes
Color the pictures.
Cut out the shapes.
Glue each shape on a Shapes Page (page 64).
Add the page to a Learning About Letters Book.

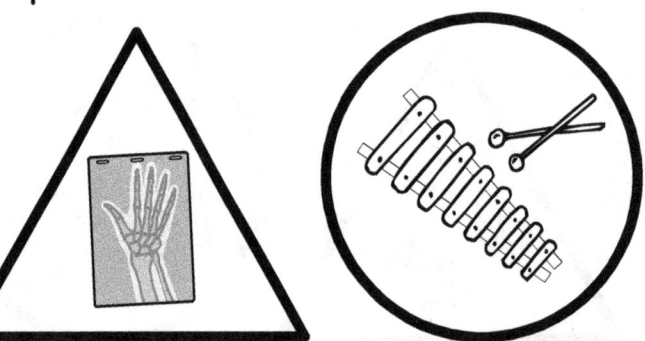
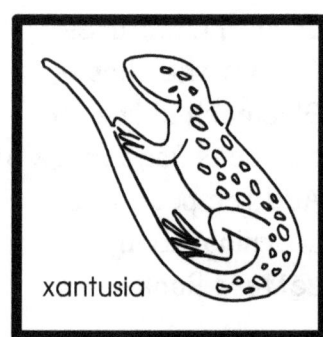

xantusia

Alphabet Picture Book Page
Trace the picture.
Color the picture.
Fill in the missing letter.
Cut out the picture.
Punch a hole at each dot.
Add the page to an Alphabet Picture Book.

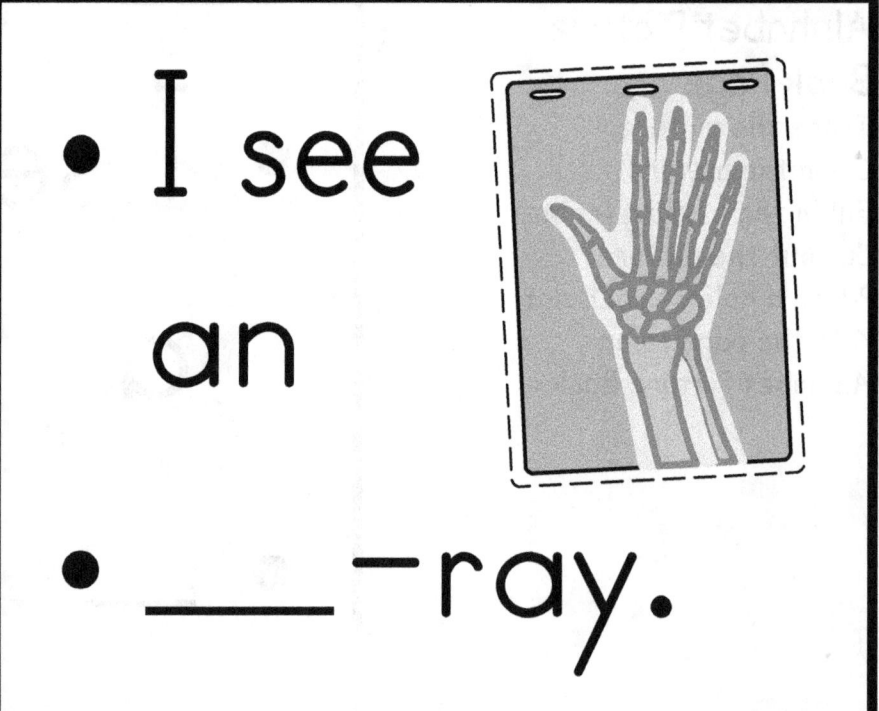

• I see an
• ___-ray.

Learning About Letter Yy

Trace the letters. Color, cut out, and glue the letter strip on a Writing Practice Page (page 64).

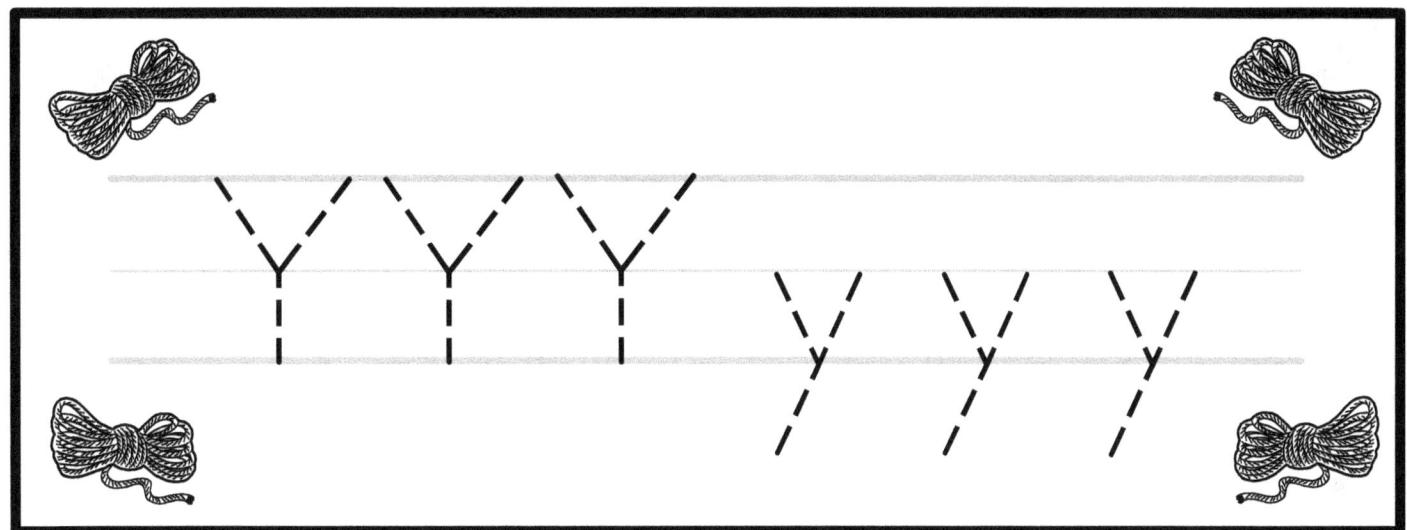

Letter Yy Picture Shapes
Color the pictures.
Cut out the shapes.
Glue each shape on
a Shapes Page (page 64).
Add the page to a
Learning About
Letters Book.

Alphabet Picture Book Page
Trace the picture.
Color the picture.
Fill in the missing letter.
Cut out the picture.
Punch a hole at each dot.
Add the page to an
Alphabet Picture Book.

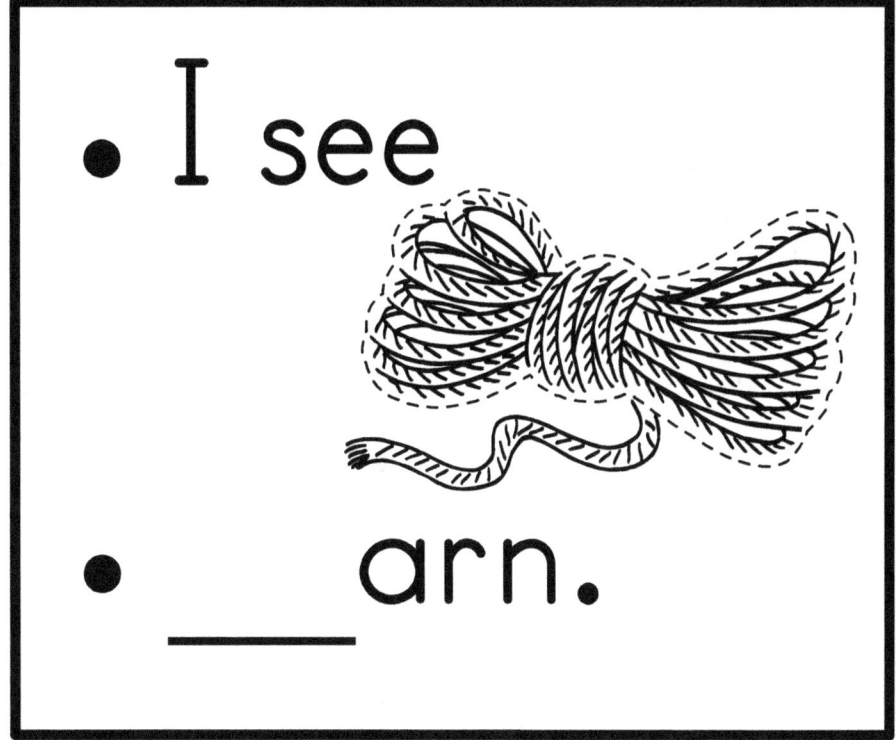

- I see

- ___arn.

Learning About Letter Zz

Trace the letters. Color, cut out, and glue the letter strip on a Writing Practice Page (page 64).

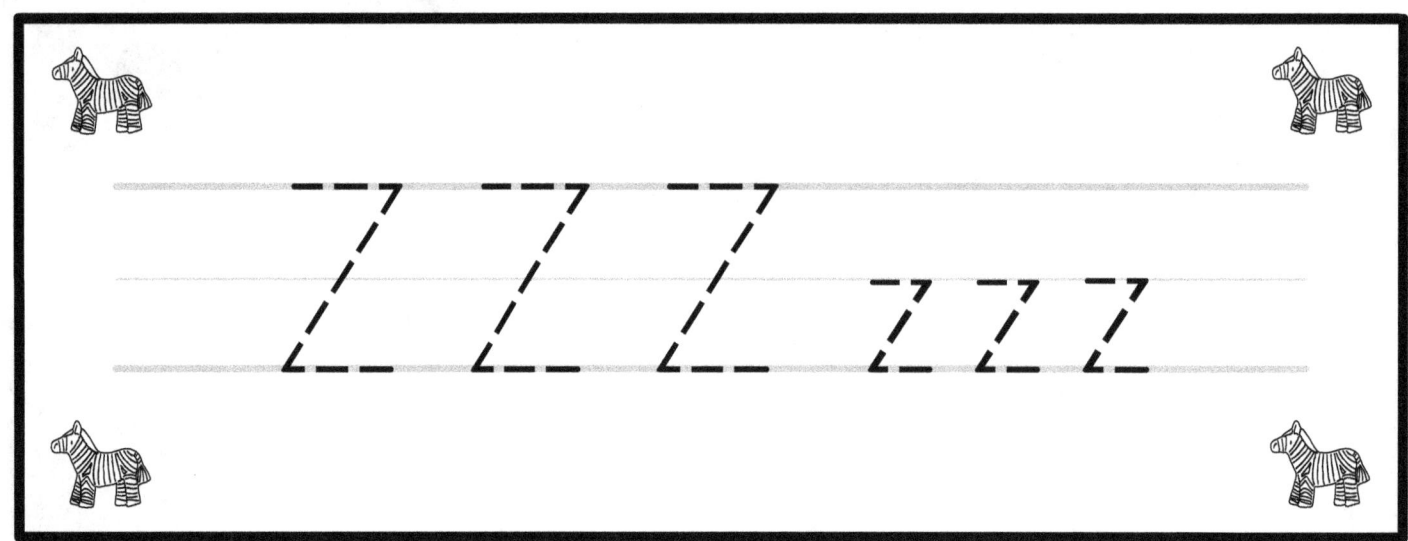

Letter Zz Picture Shapes
Color the pictures.
Cut out the shapes.
Glue each shape on
a Shapes Page (page 64).
Add the page to a
Learning About
Letters Book.

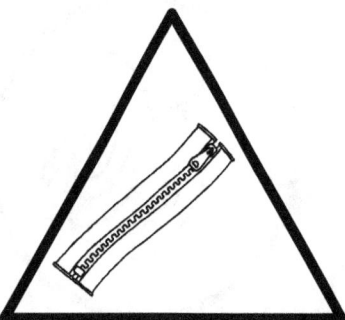

zither

Alphabet Picture Book Page
Trace the picture.
Color the picture.
Fill in the missing letter.
Cut out the picture.
Punch a hole at each dot.
Add the page to an
Alphabet Picture Book.

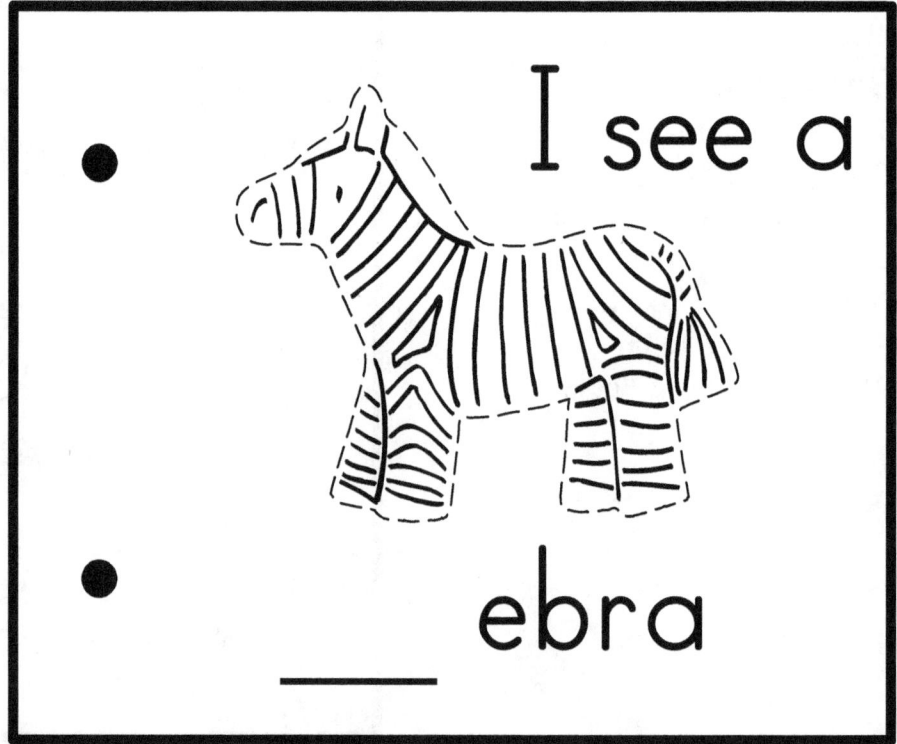

I see a

___ ebra

Learning About Number 1

Trace the numerals. Color, cut out, and glue the number strip on a Writing Practice Page (page 64).

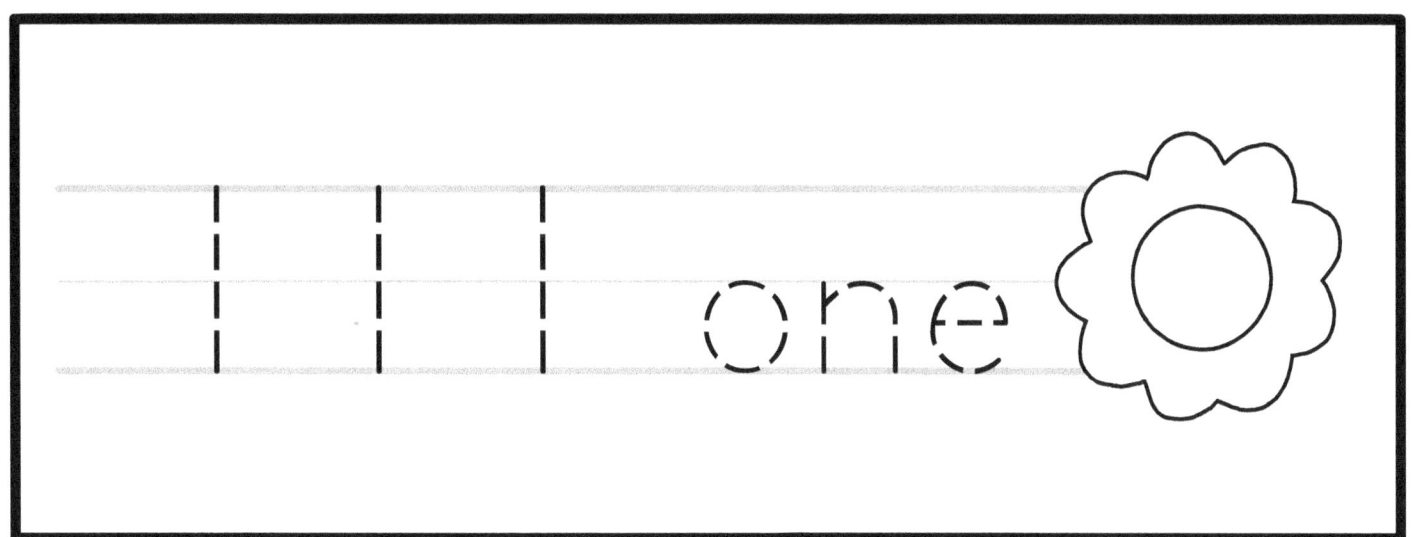

Number 1 Picture Shapes

Color the pictures.
Cut out the shapes.
Glue each shape to a Shapes Page (page 64).
Add the page to a Learning About Numbers Book.

Counting Picture Book Page

Trace the flower.
Color the picture.
Write **one** on the blank.
Cut out the picture.
Punch a hole at each dot.
Add the page to a Counting Picture Book.

Learning About Number 2

Trace the numerals. Color, cut out, and glue the number strip on a Writing Practice Page (page 64).

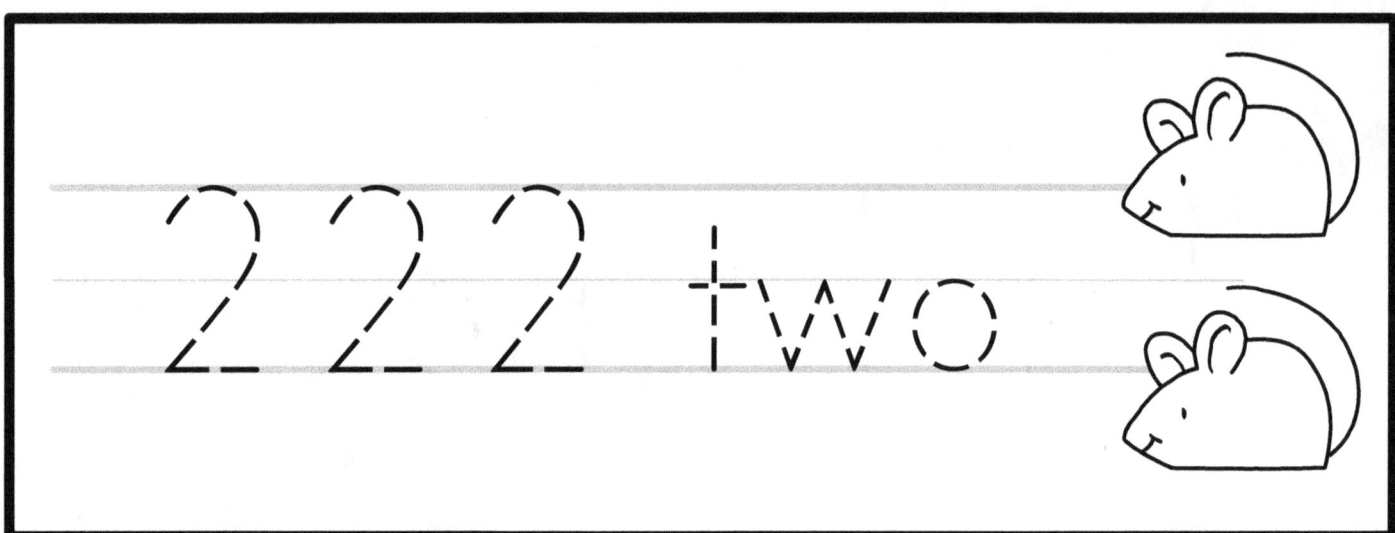

Number 2 Picture Shapes

Color the pictures.
Cut out the shapes.
Glue each shape to a
Shapes Page (page 64).
Add the page to a
Learning About
Numbers Book.

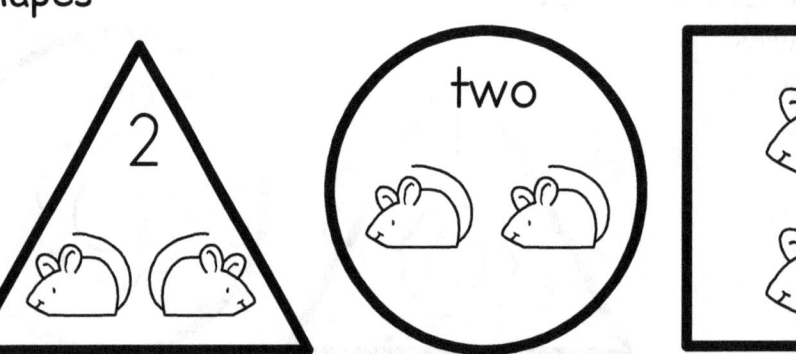 

Counting Picture Book Page

Trace the mice.
Color the picture.
Write **two** on the blank.
Cut out the picture.
Punch a hole at each dot.
Add the page to a
Counting Picture Book.

Learning About Number 3

Trace the numerals. Color, cut out, and glue the number strip on a Writing Practice Page (page 64).

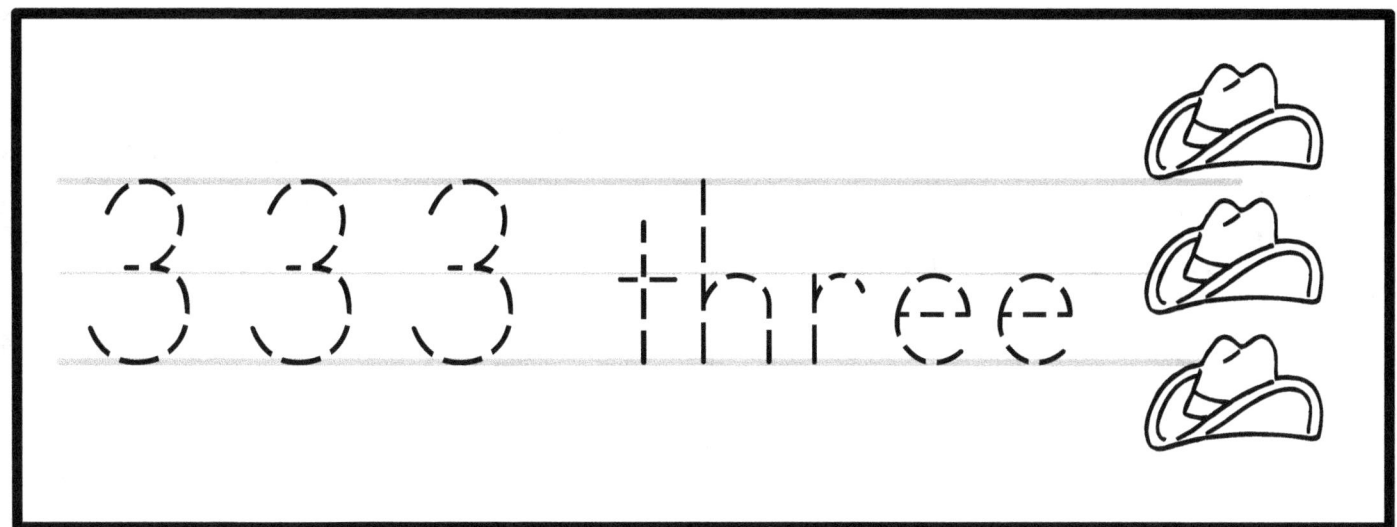

Number 3 Picture Shapes

Color the pictures.
Cut out the shapes.
Glue each shape to a
Shapes Page (page 64).
Add the page to a
Learning About
Numbers Book.

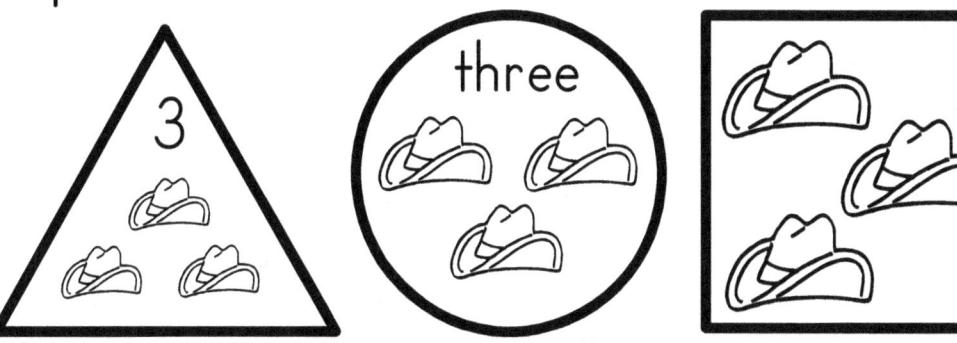

Counting Picture Book Page

Trace the hats.
Color the picture.
Write **three** on the blank.
Cut out the picture.
Punch a hole at each dot.
Add the page to a
Counting Picture Book.

Learning About Number 4

Trace the numerals. Color, cut out, and glue the number strip on a Writing Practice Page (page 64).

Number 4 Picture Shapes
Color the pictures.
Cut out the shapes.
Glue each shape to a
Shapes Page (page 64).
Add the page to a
Learning About
Numbers Book.

 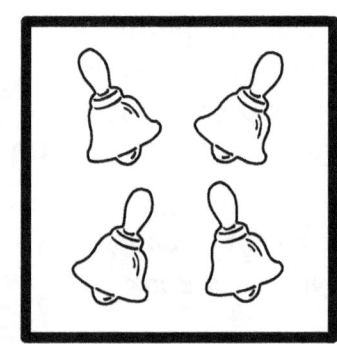

Counting Picture Book Page
Trace the bells.
Color the picture.
Write **four** on the blank.
Cut out the picture.
Punch a hole at each dot.
Add the page to a
Counting Picture Book.

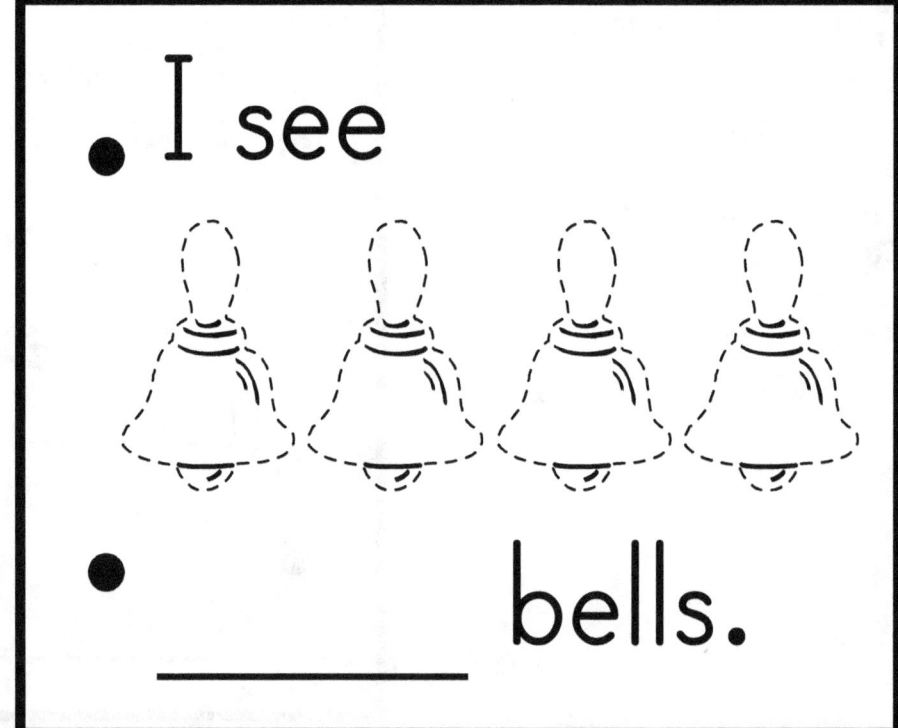

Learning About Number 5

Trace the numerals. Color, cut out, and glue the number strip on a Writing Practice Page (page 64).

Number 5 Picture Shapes
Color the pictures.
Cut out the shapes.
Glue each shape to a
Shapes Page (page 64).
Add the page to a
Learning About
Numbers Book.

Counting Picture Book Page
Trace the bats.
Color the picture.
Write **five** on the blank.
Cut out the picture.
Punch a hole at each dot.
Add the page to a
Counting Picture Book.

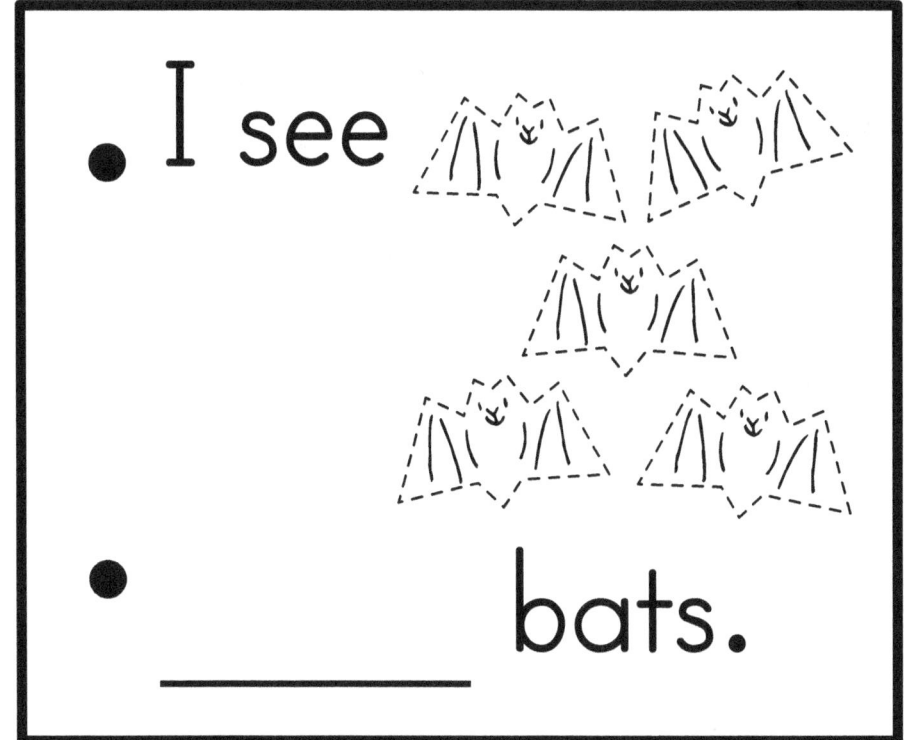

Learning About Number 6

Trace the numerals. Color, cut out, and glue the number strip on a Writing Practice Page (page 64).

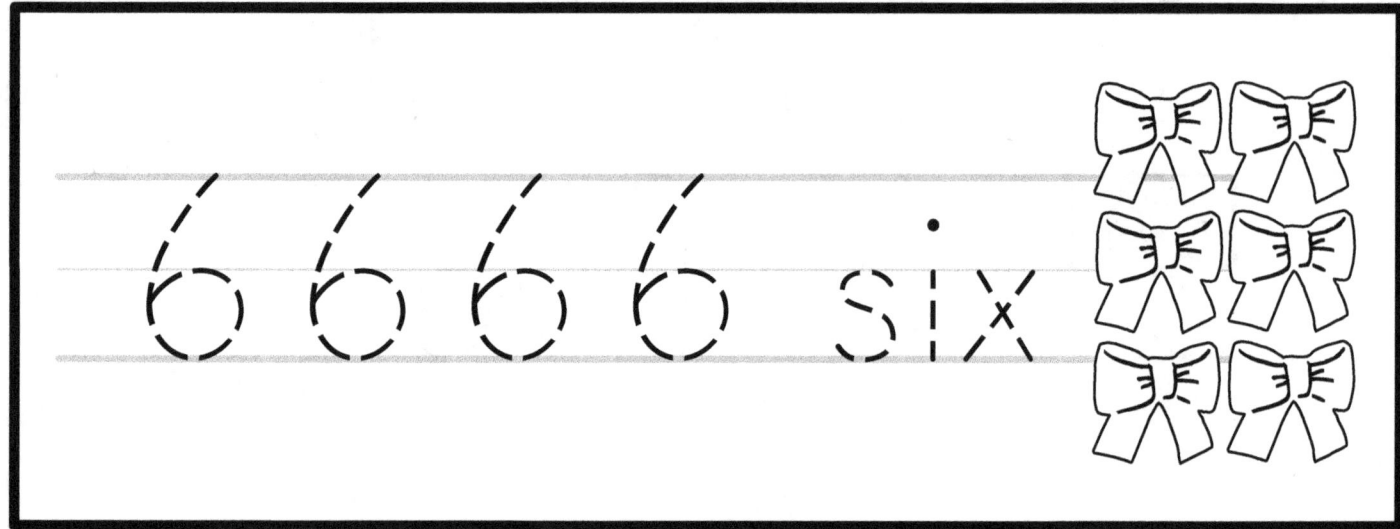

Number 6 Picture Shapes

Color the pictures.
Cut out the shapes.
Glue each shape to a
Shapes Page (page 64).
Add the page to a
Learning About
Numbers Book.

 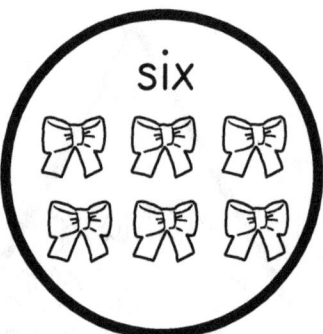 

Counting Picture Book Page

Trace the bows.
Color the picture.
Write **six** on the blank.
Cut out the picture.
Punch a hole at each dot.
Add the page to a
Counting Picture Book.

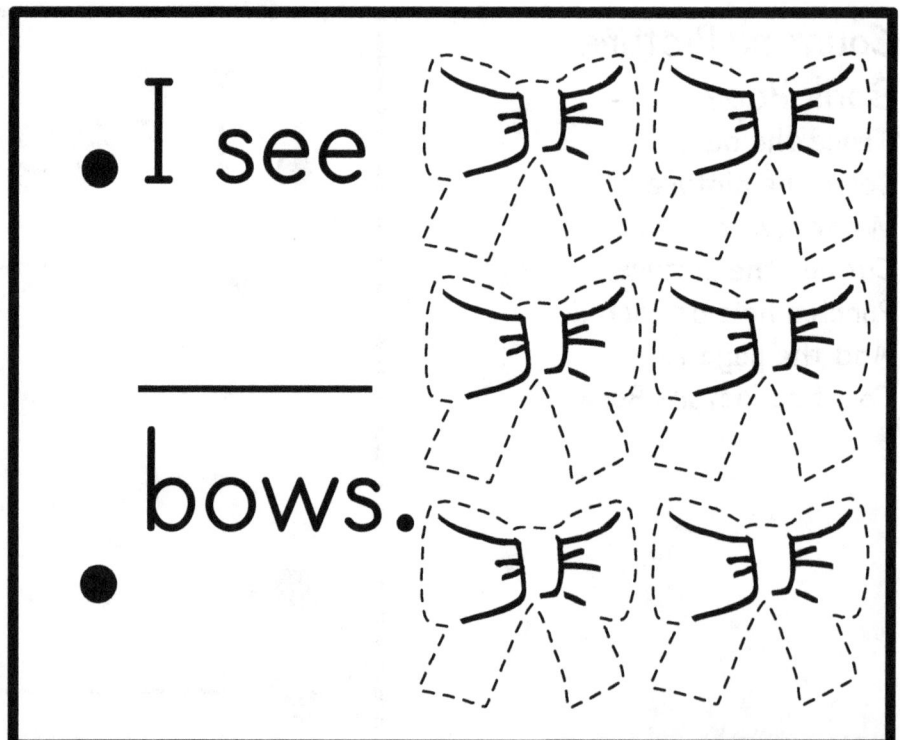

Learning About Number 7

Trace the numerals. Color, cut out, and glue the number strip on a Writing Practice Page (page 64).

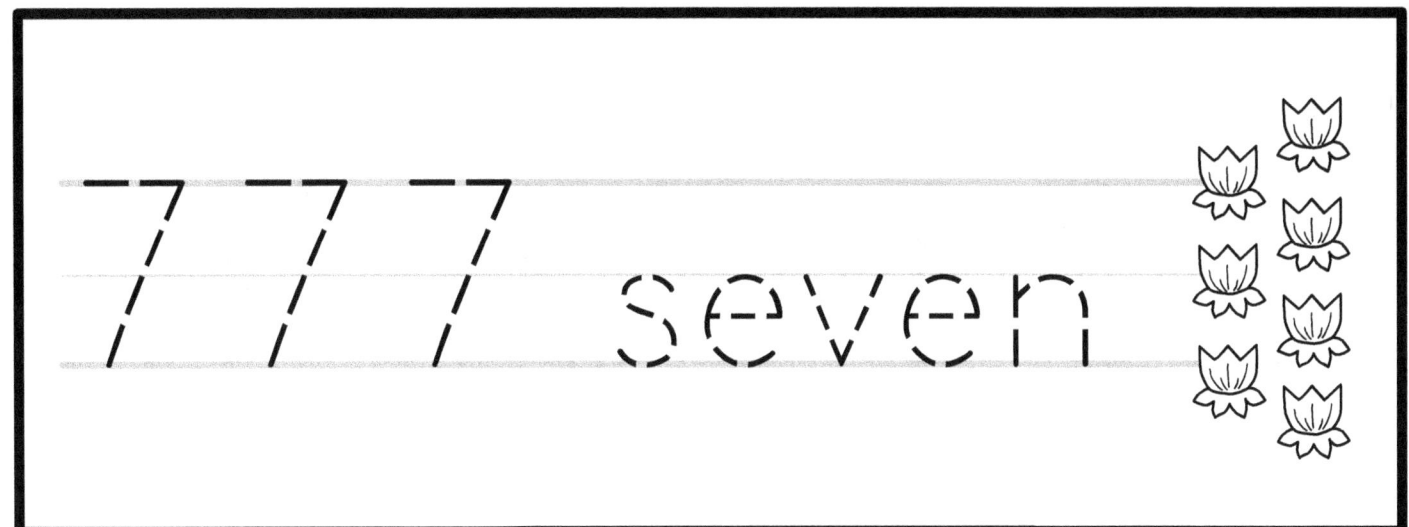

Number 7 Picture Shapes

Color the pictures.
Cut out the shapes.
Glue each shape to a
Shapes Page (page 64).
Add the page to a
Learning About
Numbers Book.

Counting Picture Book Page

Trace the flowers.
Color the picture.
Write **seven** on the blank.
Cut out the picture.
Punch a hole at each dot.
Add the page to a
Counting Picture Book.

Learning About Number 8

Trace the numerals. Color, cut out, and glue the number strip on a Writing Practice Page (page 64).

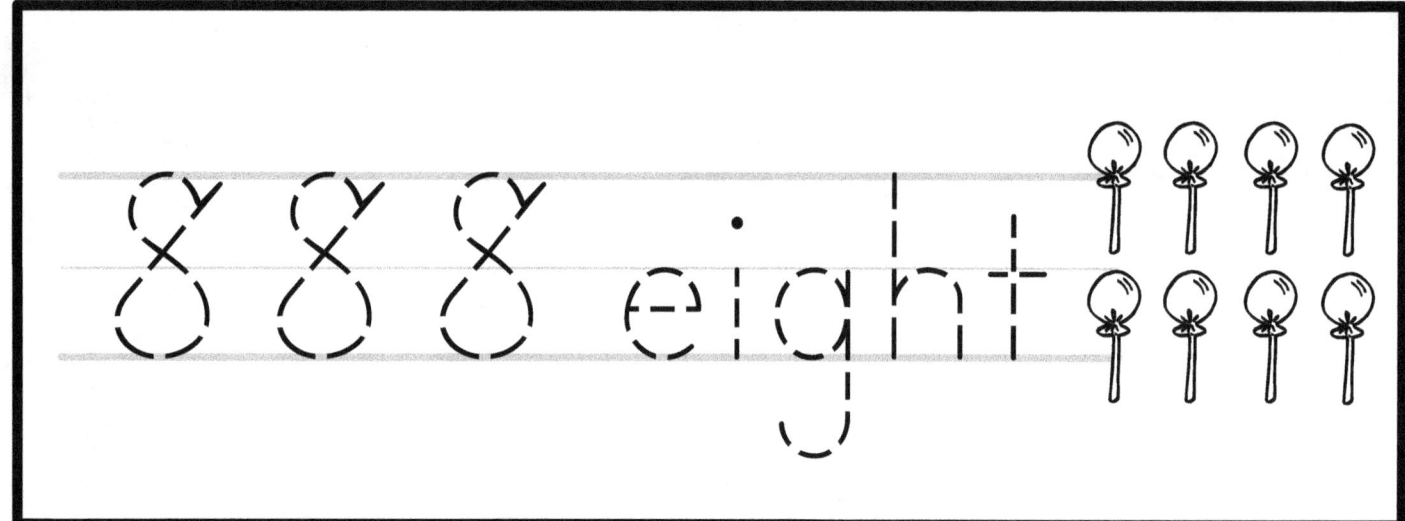

Number 8 Picture Shapes

Color the pictures.
Cut out the shapes.
Glue each shape to a
Shapes Page (page 64).
Add the page to a
Learning About
Numbers Book.

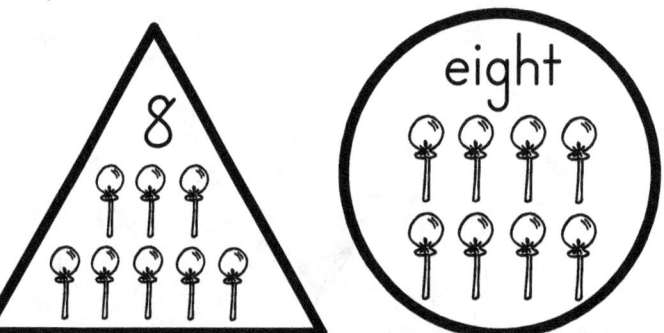 

Counting Picture Book Page

Trace the lollipops.
Color the picture.
Write **eight** on the blank.
Cut out the picture.
Punch a hole at each dot.
Add the page to a
Counting Picture Book.

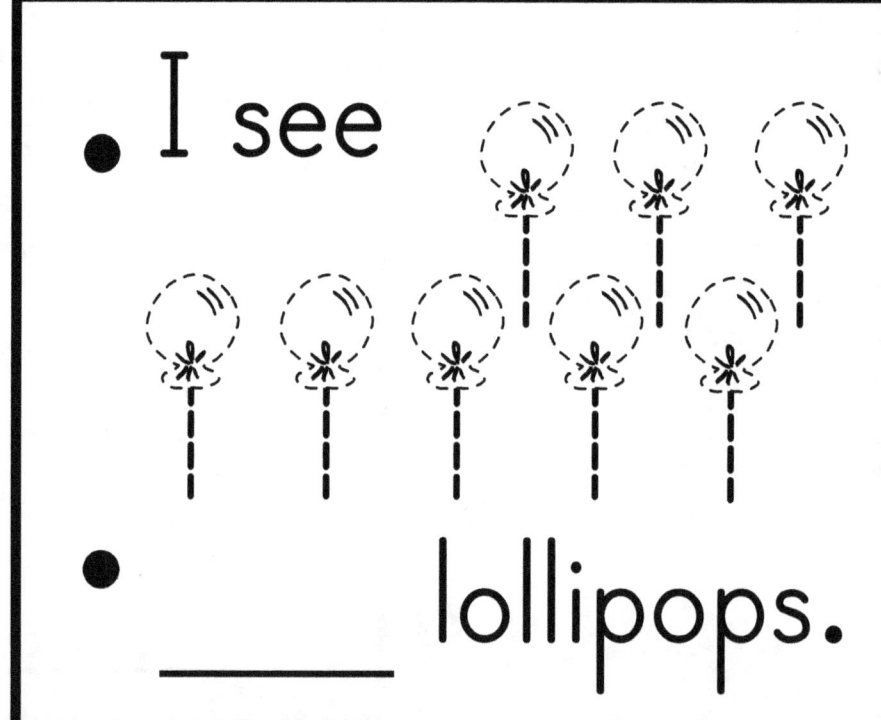

Learning About Number 9

Trace the numerals. Color, cut out, and glue the number strip on a Writing Practice Page (page 64).

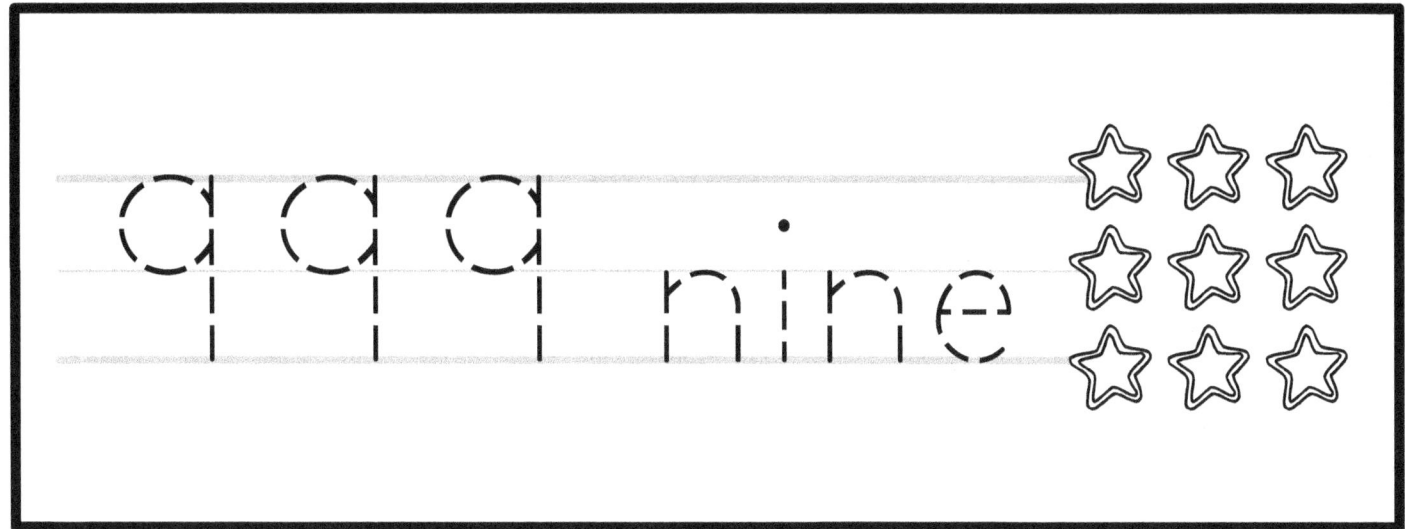

Number 9 Picture Shapes

Color the pictures.
Cut out the shapes.
Glue each shape to a Shapes Page (page 64).
Add the page to a Learning About Numbers Book.

Counting Picture Book Page

Trace the stars.
Color the picture.
Write **nine** on the blank.
Cut out the picture.
Punch a hole at each dot.
Add the page to a Counting Picture Book.

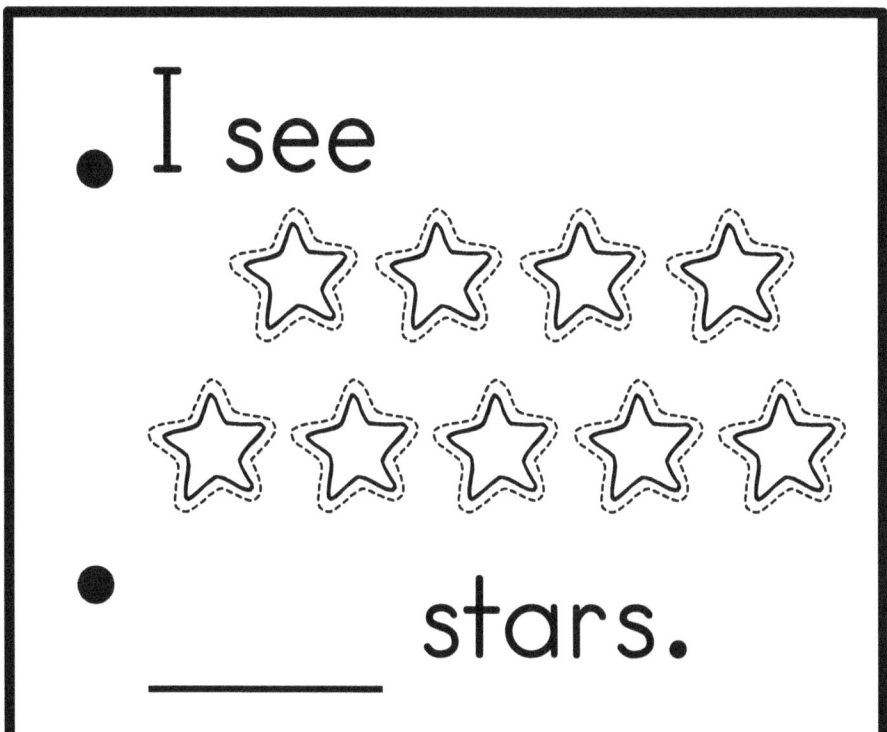

Learning About Number 10

Trace the numerals. Color, cut out, and glue the number strip on a Writing Practice Page (page 64).

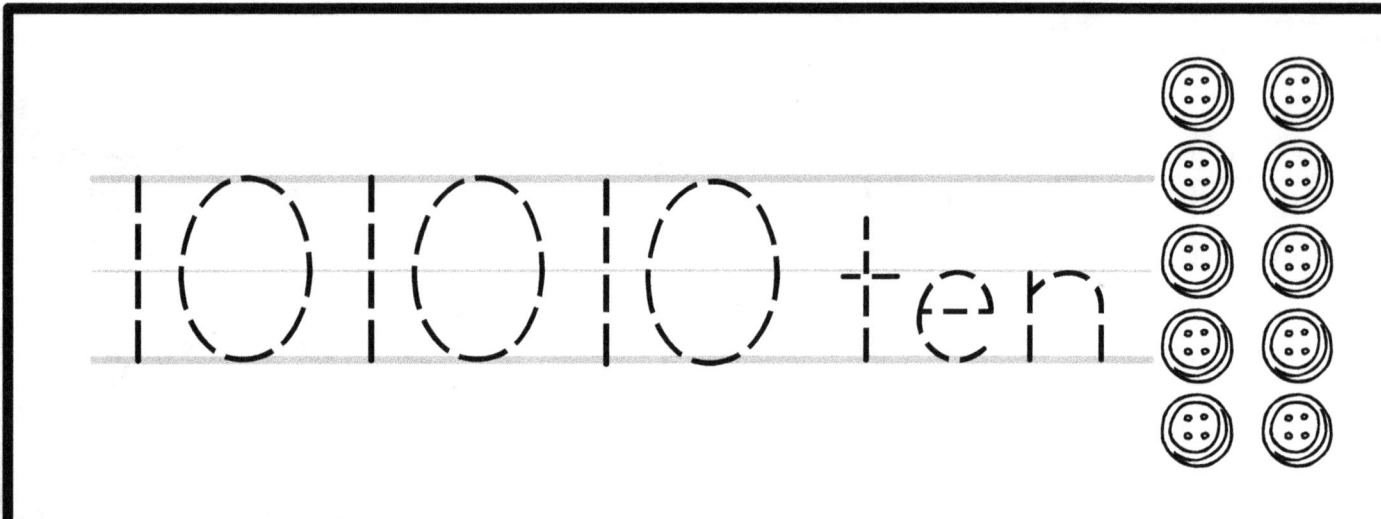

Number 10 Picture Shapes

Color the pictures.
Cut out the shapes.
Glue each shape to a Shapes Page (page 64).
Add the page to a Learning About Numbers Book.

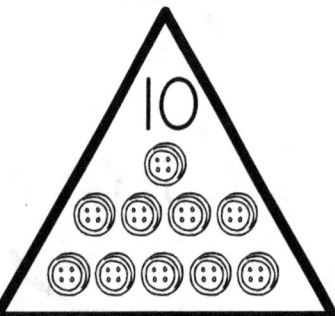 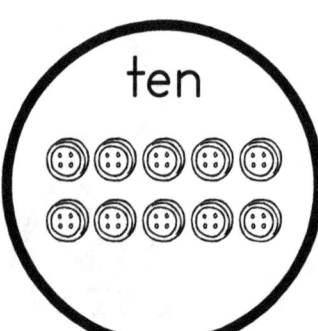 

Counting Picture Book Page

Trace the buttons.
Color the picture.
Write **ten** on the blank.
Cut out the picture.
Punch a hole at each dot.
Add the page to a Counting Picture Book.

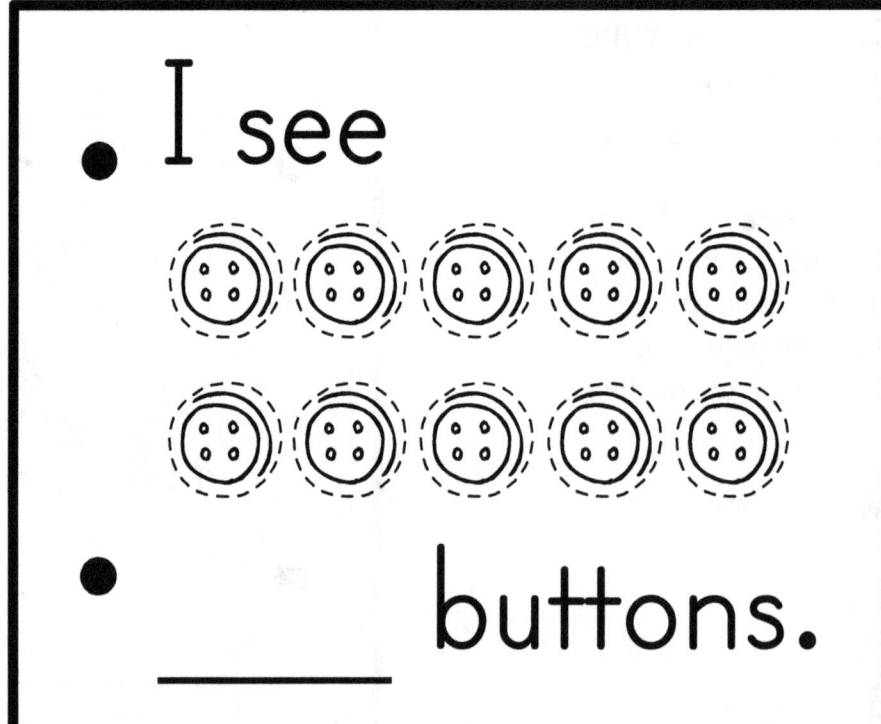

Connect-the-Letters
Connect Letters a through m

Start at letter **a** to connect the dots. Color the picture.
Cut out and glue the picture on a sheet of construction paper.

Options:
- Use glue and yarn to connect the dots.
- Punch two holes, then lace and tie a length of yarn at the top of the cutout to form a hanging picture.

Connect-the-Letters
Connect Letters a through m

Start at letter **a** to connect the dots. Color the picture.
Cut out and glue the picture on a sheet of construction paper.

Options:
- Use glue and yarn to connect the dots.
- Punch two holes, then lace and tie a length of yarn at the top of the cutout to form a hanging picture.

Connect-the-Letters
Connect Letters n through z

Start at letter **n** to connect the dots. Color the picture.
Cut out and glue the picture on a sheet of construction paper.

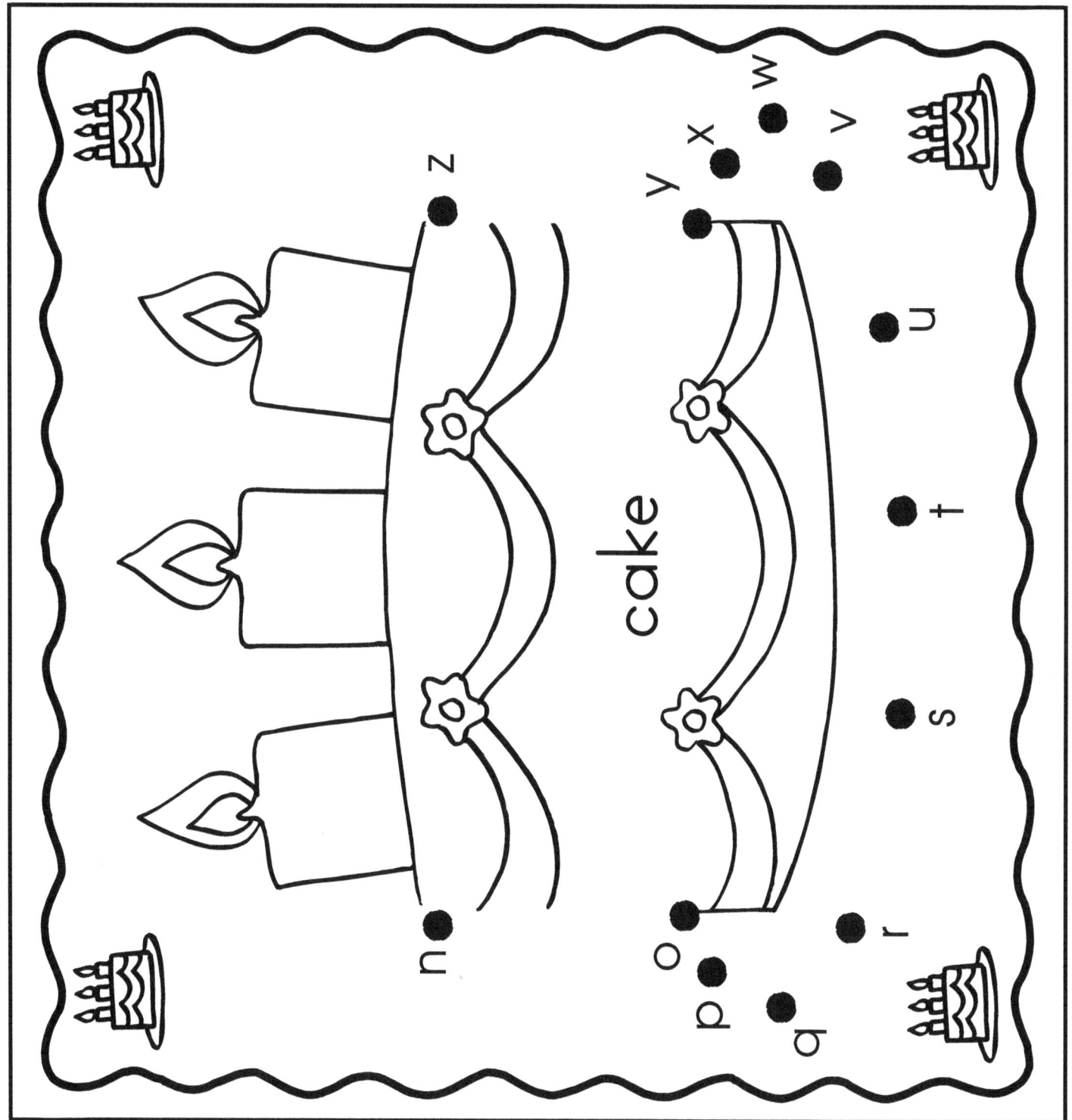

Options:
- Use glue and yarn to connect the dots.
- Punch two holes, then lace and tie a length of yarn at the top of the cutout to form a hanging picture.

LAB20132 • SCRIBBLE SCRIBBLE • 978-1-937257-19-4
©2013 Little Acorn Books™

Connect-the-Letters
Connect Letters n through z

Start at letter **n** to connect the dots. Color the picture.
Cut out and glue the picture on a sheet of construction paper.

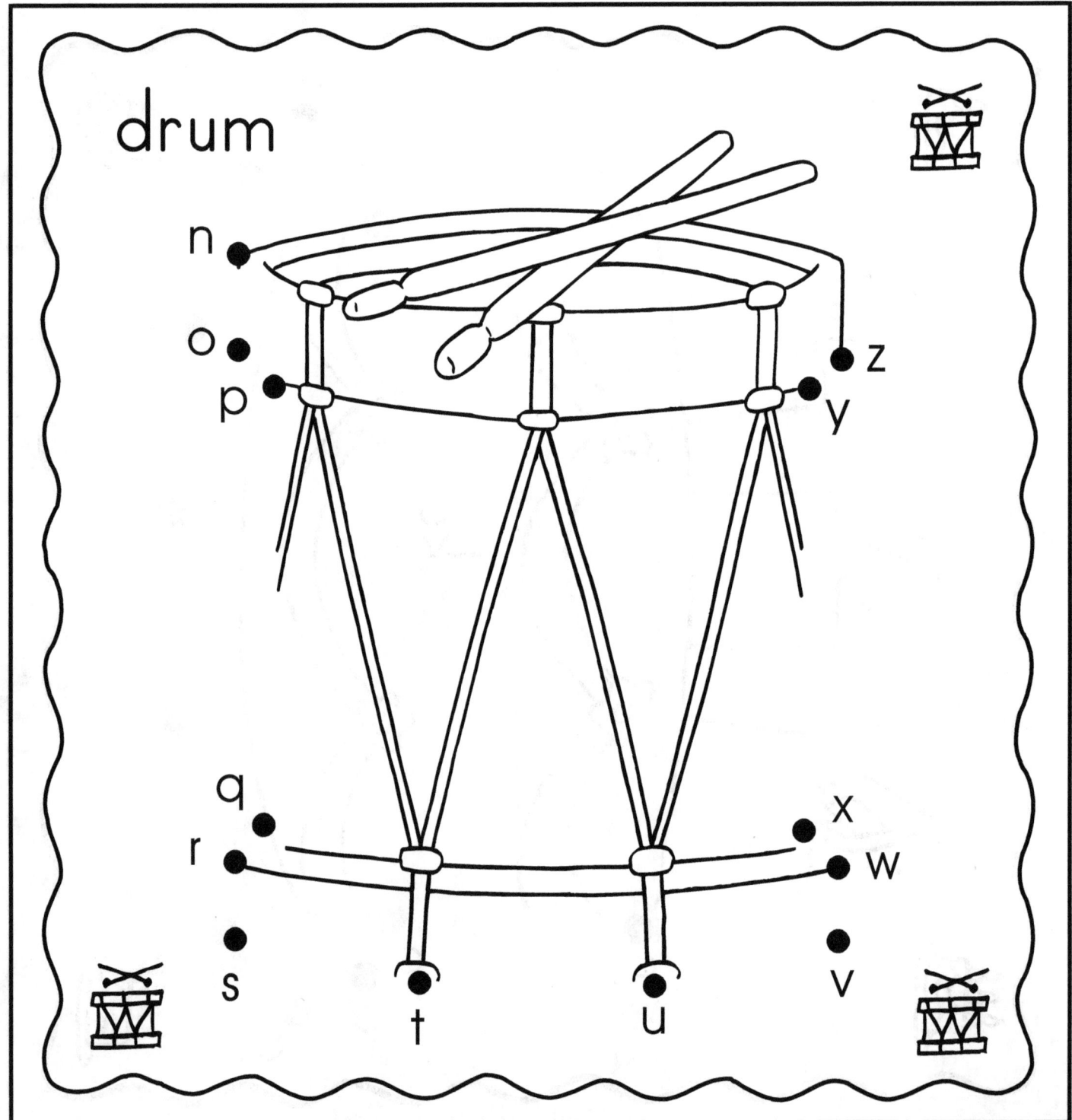

Options:
- Cut and glue yarn on the drum.
- Punch two holes, then lace and tie a length of yarn at the top of the cutout to form a hanging picture.

Connect-the-Letters
Connect Letters A through M

Start at letter **A** to connect the dots. Color the picture.
Cut out and glue the picture on a sheet of construction paper.

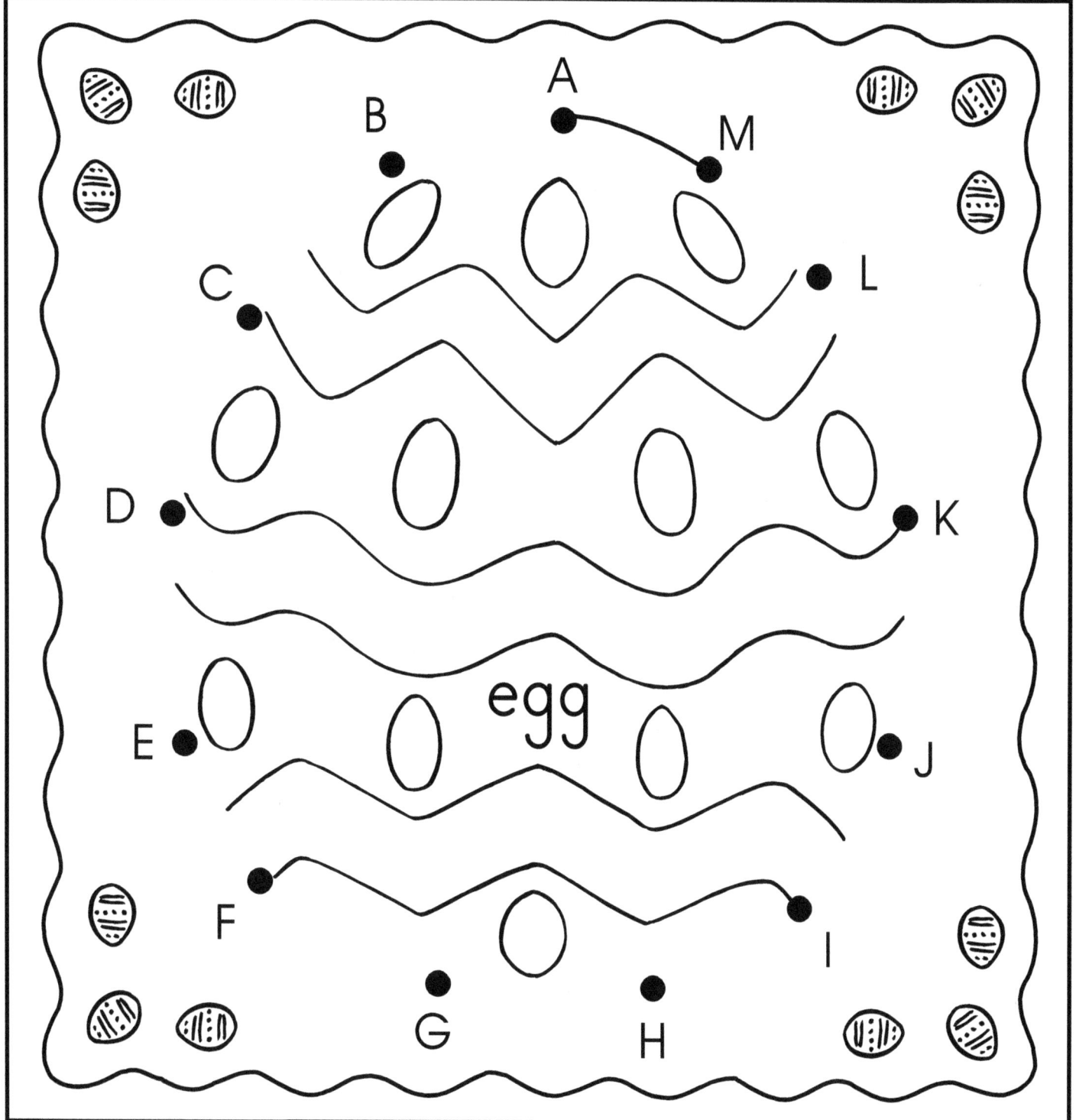

Options:
- Decorate the egg with glitter, beans, beads, and small pom poms.
- Punch two holes, then lace and tie a length of yarn at the top of the cutout to form a hanging picture.

Connect-the-Letters
Connect Letters A through M

Start at letter **A** to connect the dots. Color the picture.
Cut out and glue the picture on a sheet of construction paper.

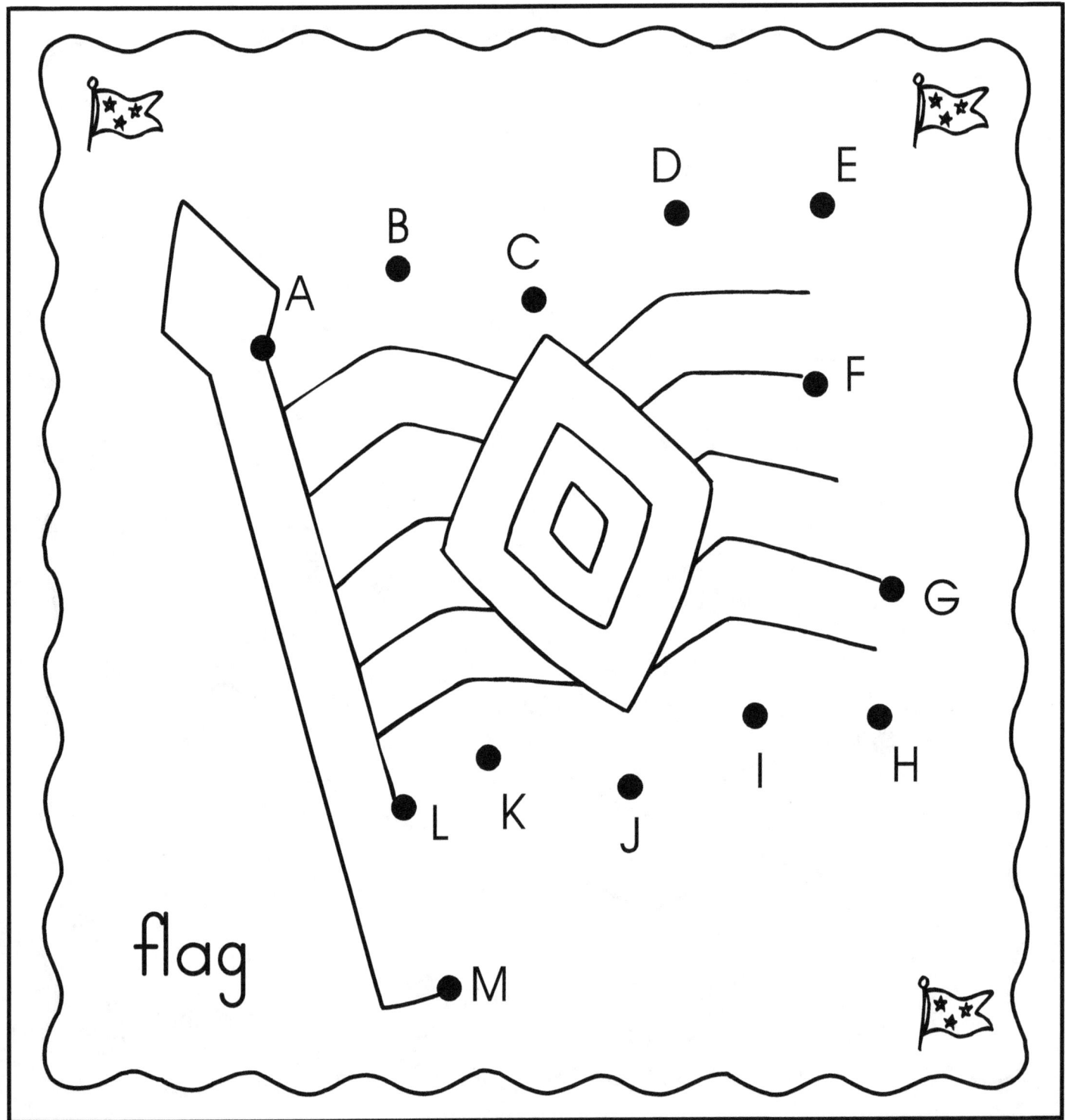

Options:
- Cut and glue yarn on the flag.
- Punch two holes, then lace and tie a length of yarn at the top of the cutout to form a hanging picture.

Connect-the-Letters
Connect Letters N through Z

Start at letter **N** to connect the dots. Color the picture.
Cut out and glue the picture on a sheet of construction paper.

Options:
- Reproduce the ghost on black construction paper. Color the ghost with chalk.
- Punch two holes, then lace and tie a length of yarn at the top of the cutout to form a hanging picture.

Connect-the-Letters
Connect Letters N through Z

Start at letter **N** to connect the dots. Color the picture.
Cut out and glue the picture on a sheet of construction paper.

Options:
- Cut, tie, then glue a ribbon bow on the heart.
- Punch two holes, then lace and tie a length of yarn at the top of the cutout to form a hanging picture.

Connect-the-Letters
Connect Letters a through z

Start at letter **a** to connect the dots. Color the picture.
Cut out and glue the picture on a sheet of construction paper.

Options:
- Glue glitter sprinkles on top of the ice cream.
- Punch two holes, then lace and tie a length of yarn at the top of the cutout to form a hanging picture.

Connect-the-Letters
Connect Letters a through z

Start at letter **a** to connect the dots. Color the picture.
Cut out and glue the picture on a sheet of construction paper.

Options:
- Trace, cut, and glue yellow cellophane on the jar.
- Punch two holes, then lace and tie a length of yarn at the top of the cutout to form a hanging picture.

Connect-the-Letters
Connect Letters A through Z

Start at letter **A** to connect the dots. Color the picture.
Cut out and glue the picture on a sheet of construction paper.

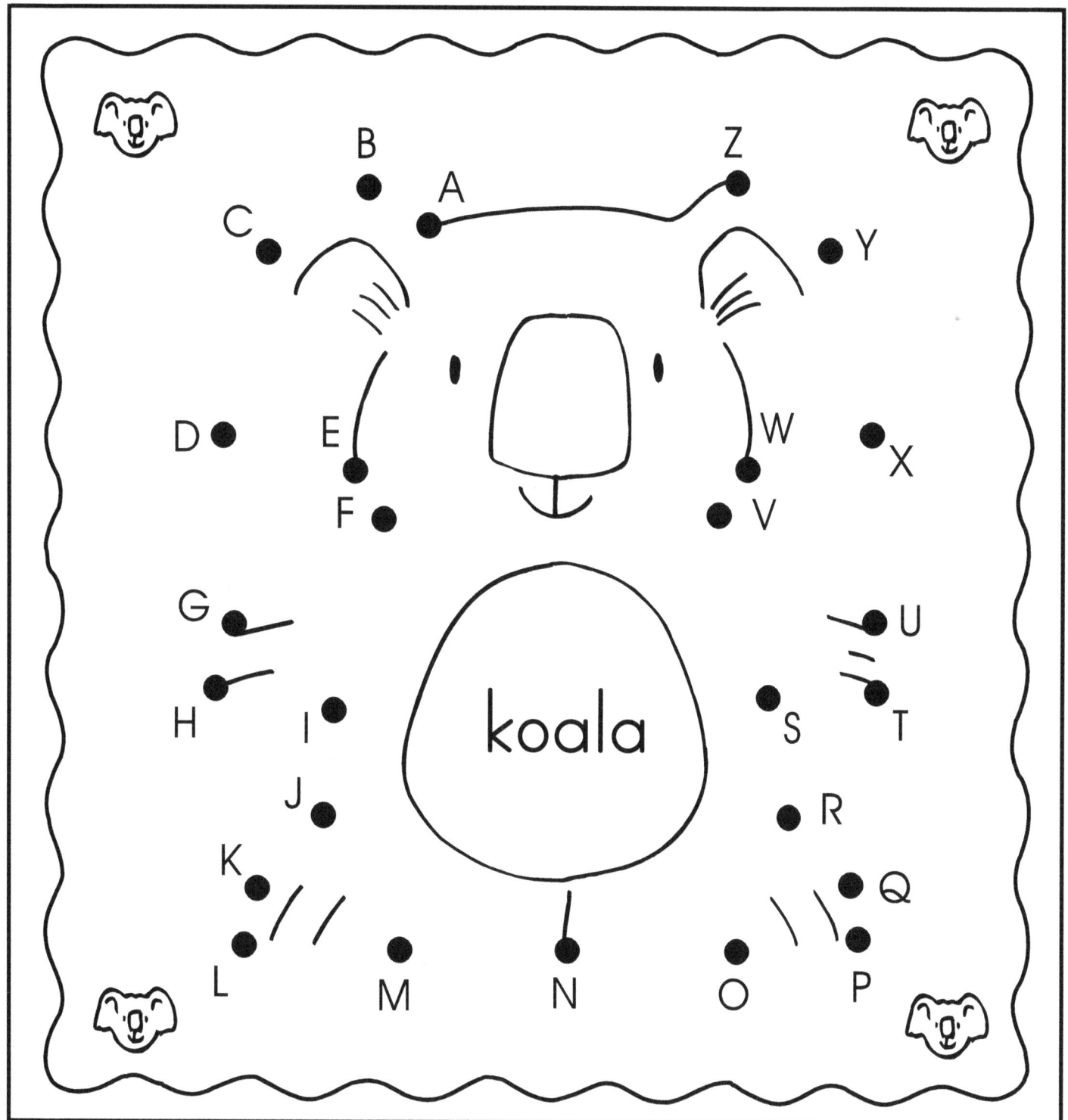

Options:
- Use glue and gray yarn to connect the dots.
- Punch two holes, then lace and tie a length of yarn at the top of the cutout to form a hanging picture.

Connect-the-Letters
Connect Letters A through Z

Start at letter **A** to connect the dots. Color the picture.
Cut out and glue the picture on a sheet of construction paper.

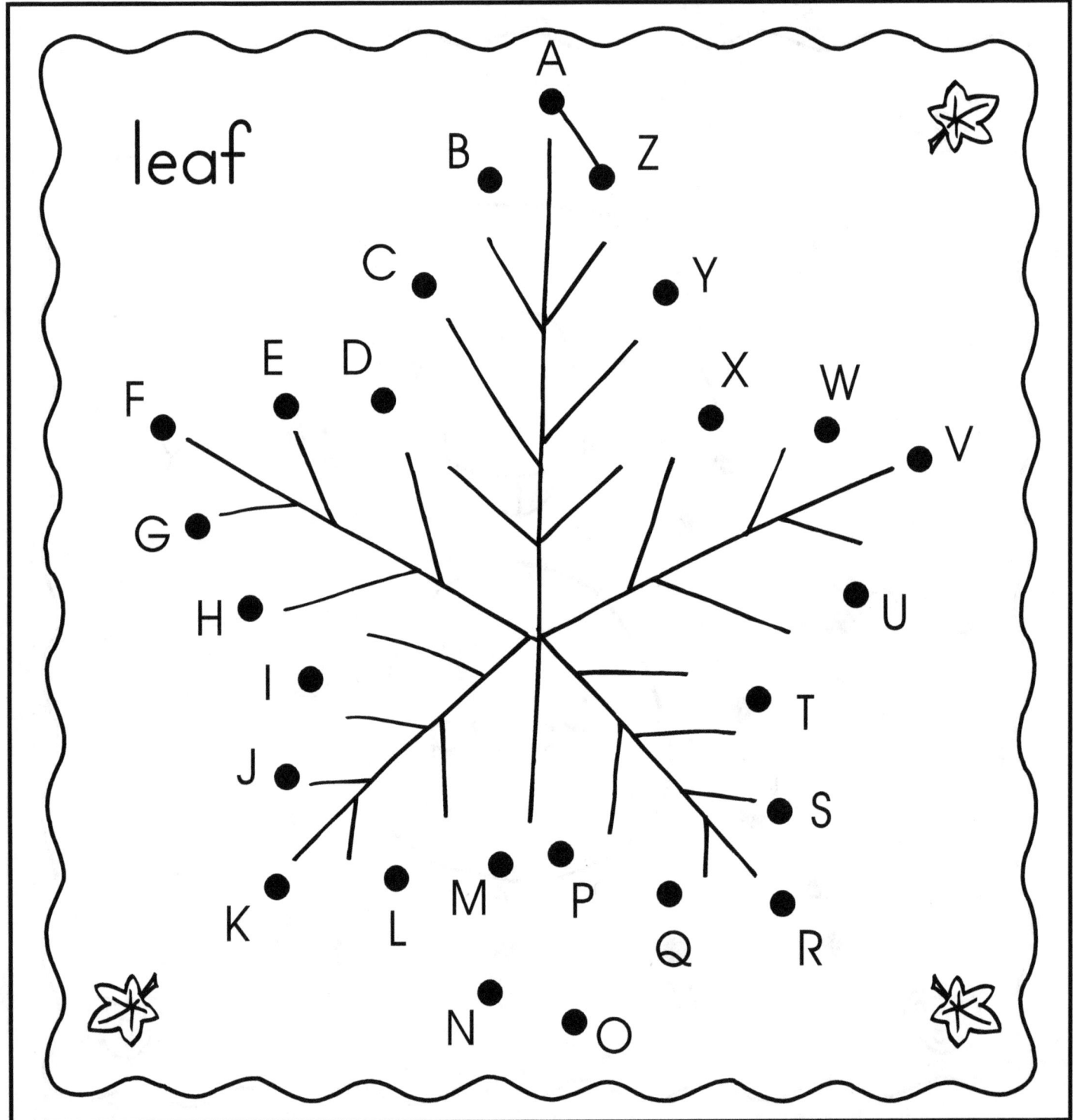

Options:
- Use glue and yarn to connect the dots.
- Punch two holes, then lace and tie a length of yarn at the top of the cutout to form a hanging picture.

Connect-the-Letters
Connect Letters A through Z

Start at letter **A** to connect the dots. Color the picture.
Cut out and glue the picture on a sheet of construction paper.

Options:
- Paint on glue then sprinkle glitter on the stars.
- Punch two holes, then lace and tie a length of yarn at the top of the cutout to form a hanging picture.

Connect-the-Numbers
Connect Numbers 1 through 10

Start at number **1** to connect the dots. Color the picture.
Cut out and glue the picture on a sheet of construction paper.

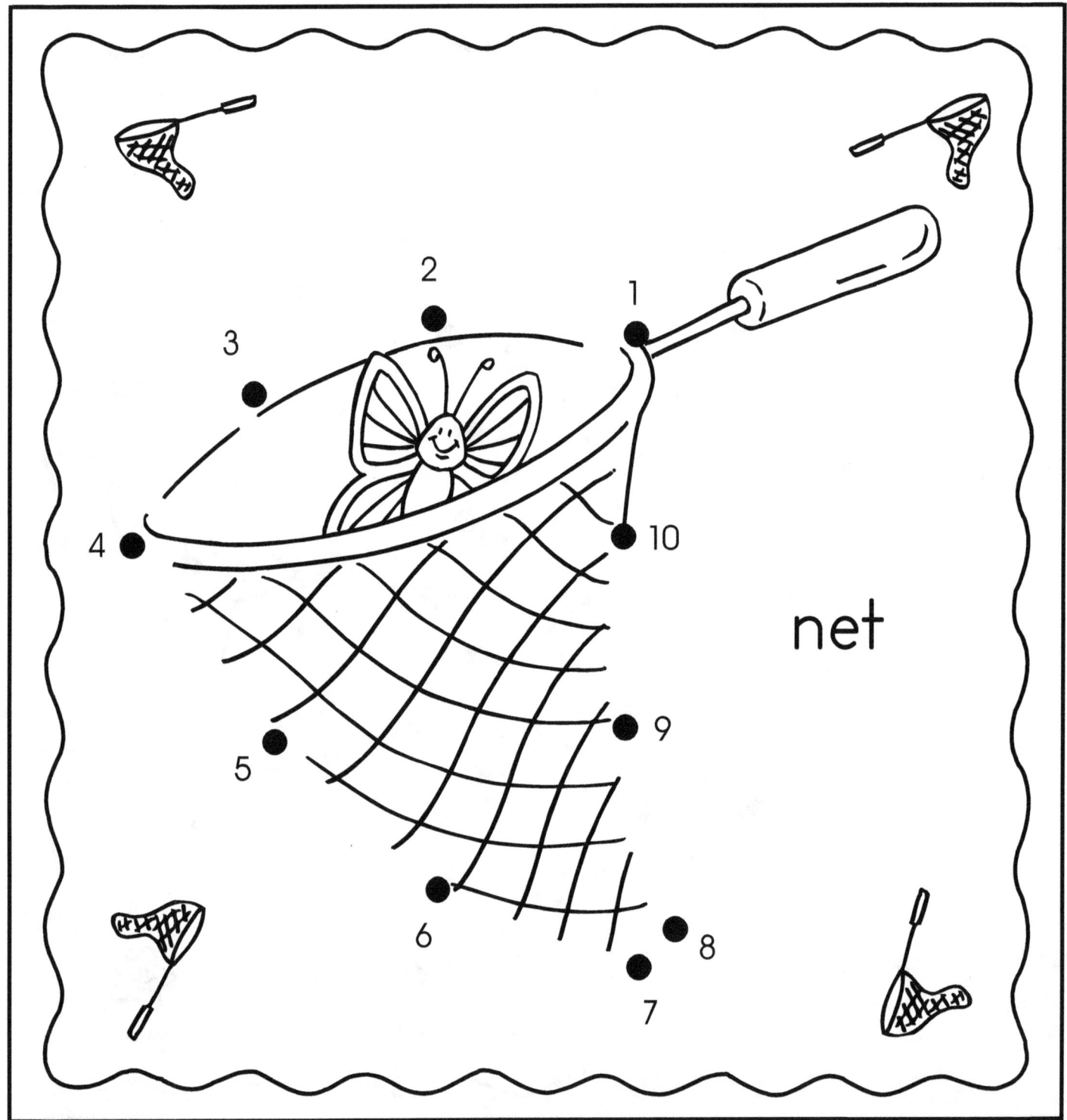

net

Options:
- Cut out and glue construction paper butterflies around the net.
- Punch two holes, then lace and tie a length of yarn at the top of the cutout to form a hanging picture.

Connect-the-Numbers
Connect Numbers 1 through 10

Start at number **1** to connect the dots. Color the picture.
Cut out and glue the picture on a sheet of construction paper.

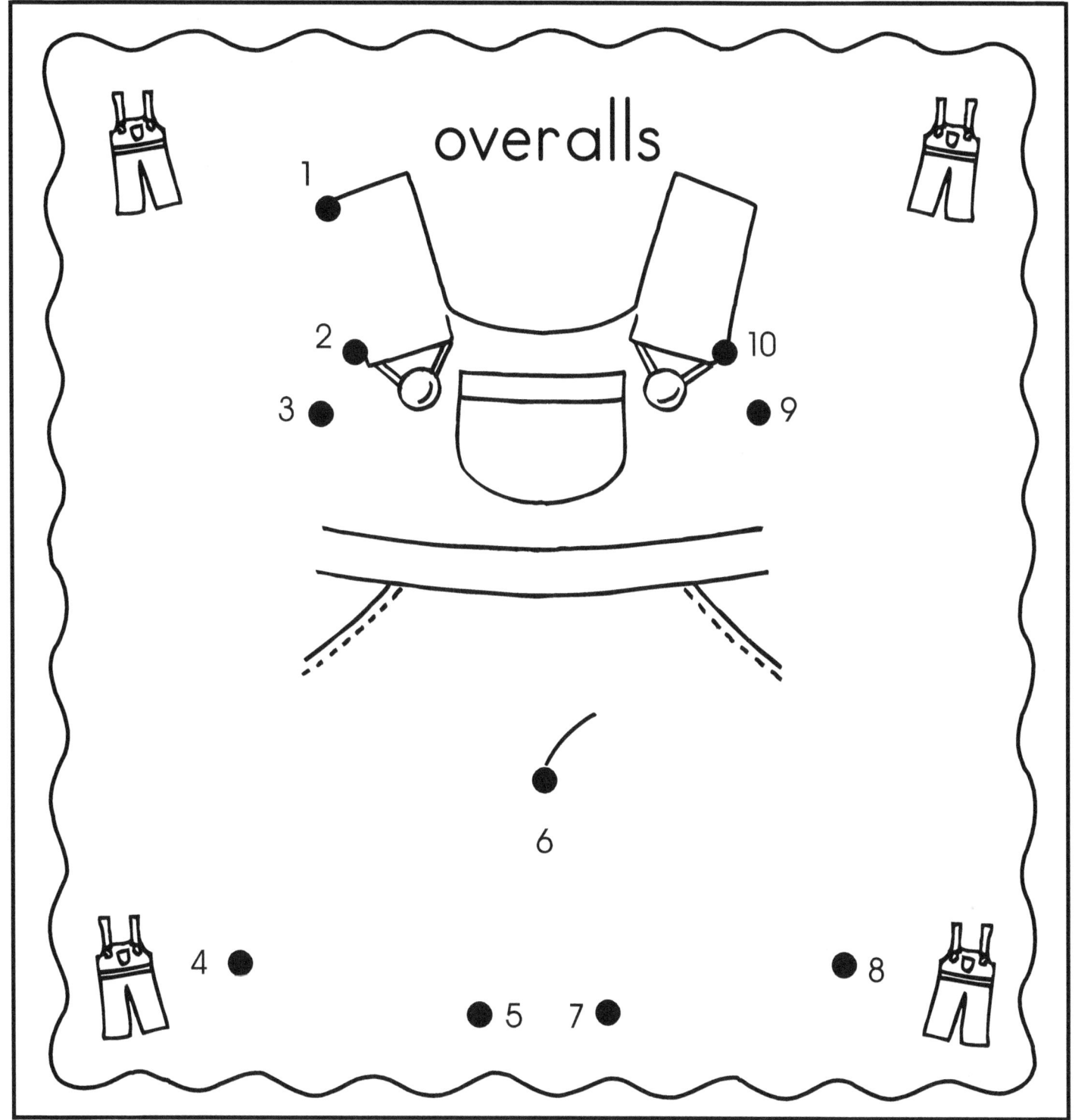

Options:
- Cut and glue cloth patches on the overalls.
- Punch two holes, then lace and tie a length of yarn at the top of the cutout to form a hanging picture.

Connect-the-Numbers
Connect Numbers 1 through 10

Start at number **1** to connect the dots. Color the picture.
Cut out and glue the picture on a sheet of construction paper.

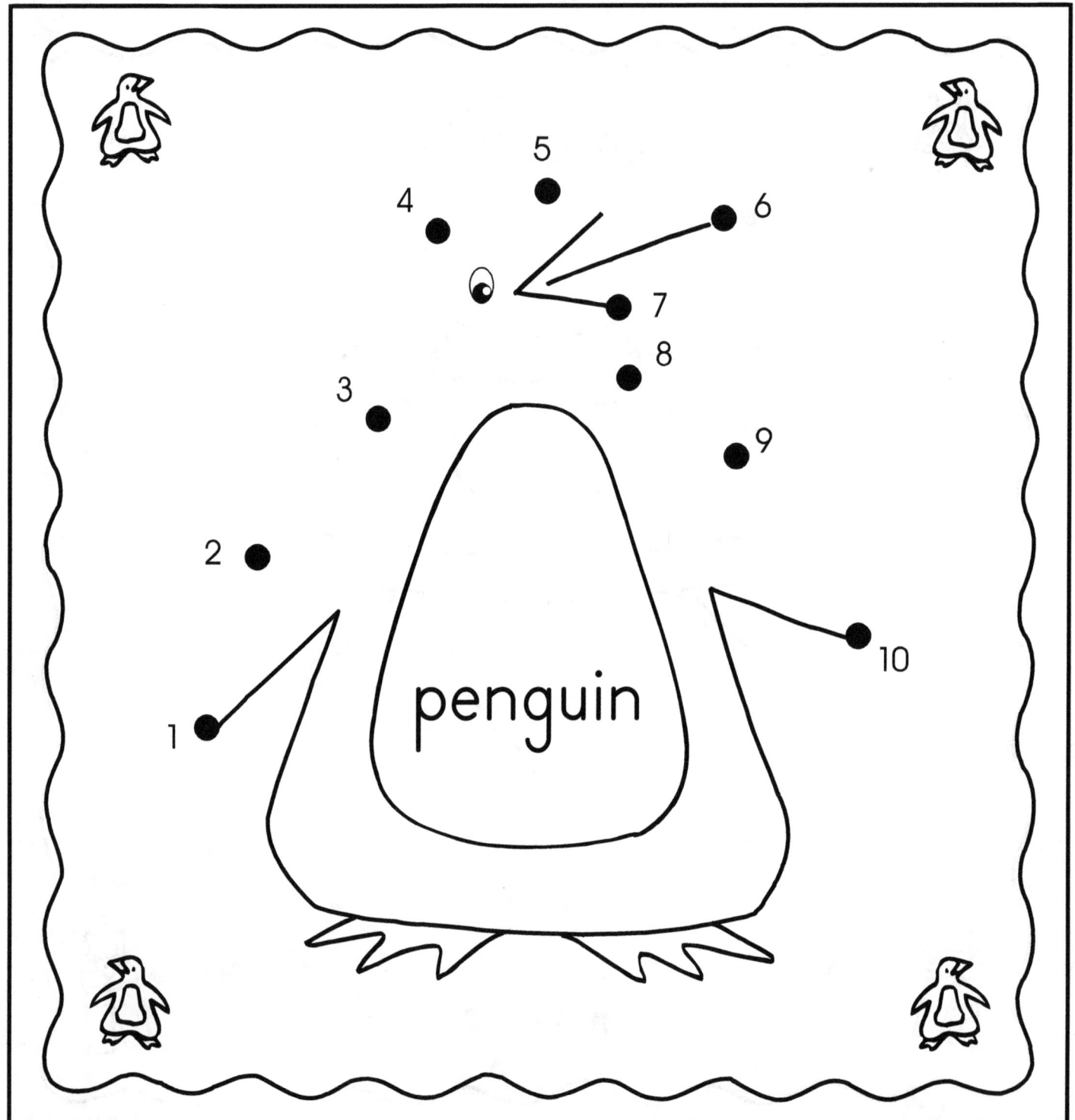

Options:
- Use glue and black yarn to connect the dots.
- Punch two holes, then lace and tie a length of yarn at the top of the cutout to form a hanging picture.

Connect-the-Numbers
Connect Numbers 1 through 10

Start at number **1** to connect the dots. Color the picture.
Cut out and glue the picture on a sheet of construction paper.

Options:
- Glue sequins on the queen's crown and robe.
- Punch two holes, then lace and tie a length of yarn at the top of the cutout to form a hanging picture.

Connect-the-Numbers
Connect Numbers 1 through 10

Start at number **1** to connect the dots. Color the picture.
Cut out and glue the picture on a sheet of construction paper.

Options:
- Glue sequins and buttons on the robot.
- Punch two holes, then lace and tie a length of yarn at the top of the cutout to form a hanging picture.

Connect-the-Numbers
Connect Numbers 1 through 20

Start at number **1** to connect the dots. Color the picture.
Cut out and glue the picture on a sheet of construction paper.

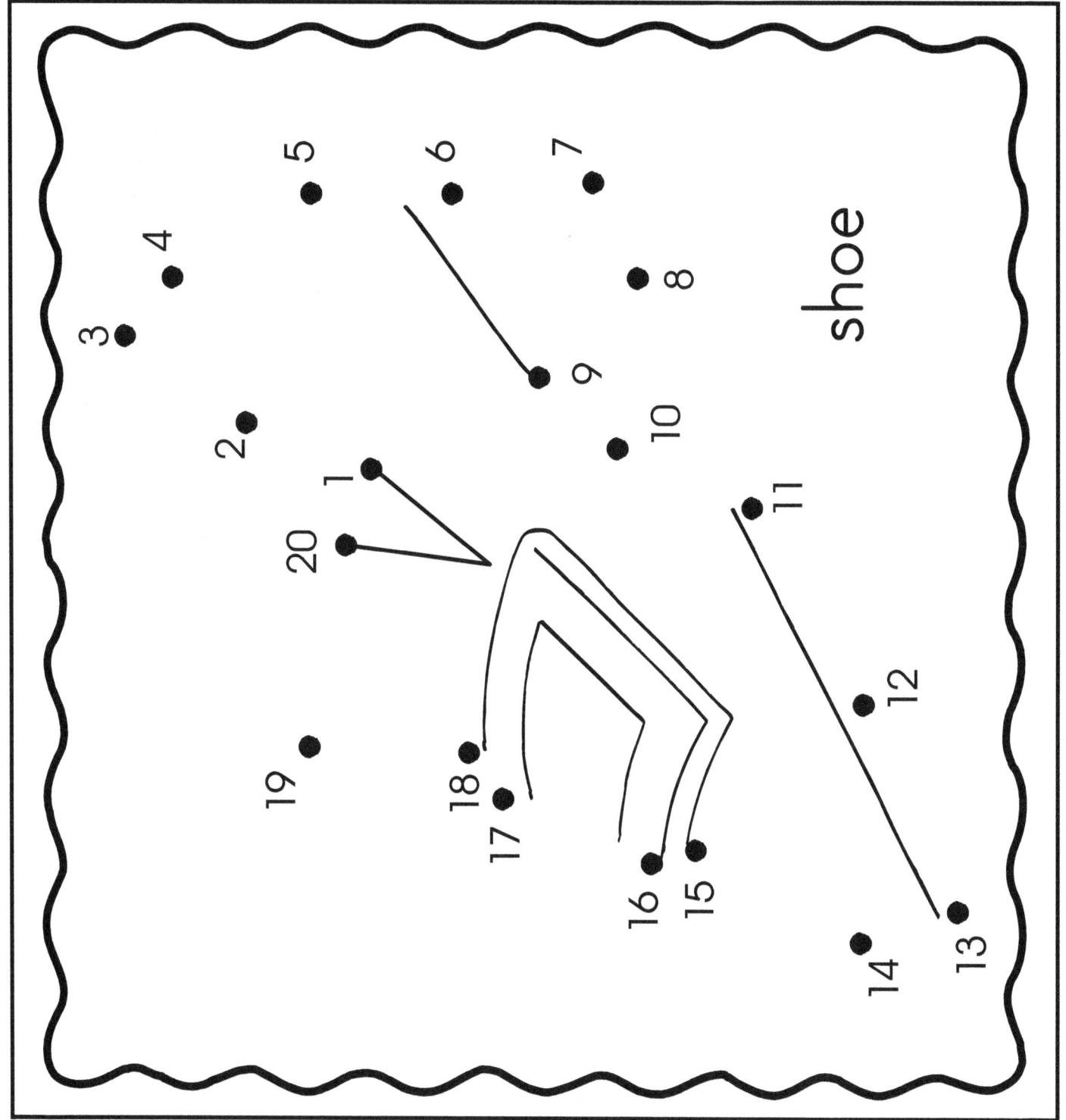

Options:
- Use glue and yarn to connect the dots.
- Punch two holes, then lace and tie a length of yarn at the top of the cutout to form a hanging picture.

Connect-the-Numbers
Connect Numbers 1 through 20

Start at number **1** to connect the dots. Color the picture.
Cut out and glue the picture on a sheet of construction paper.

Options:
- Use glue and yarn to connect the dots.
- Punch two holes, then lace and tie a length of yarn at the top of the cutout to form a hanging picture.

Connect-the-Numbers
Connect Numbers 1 through 20

Start at number **1** to connect the dots. Color the picture.
Cut out and glue the picture on a sheet of construction paper.

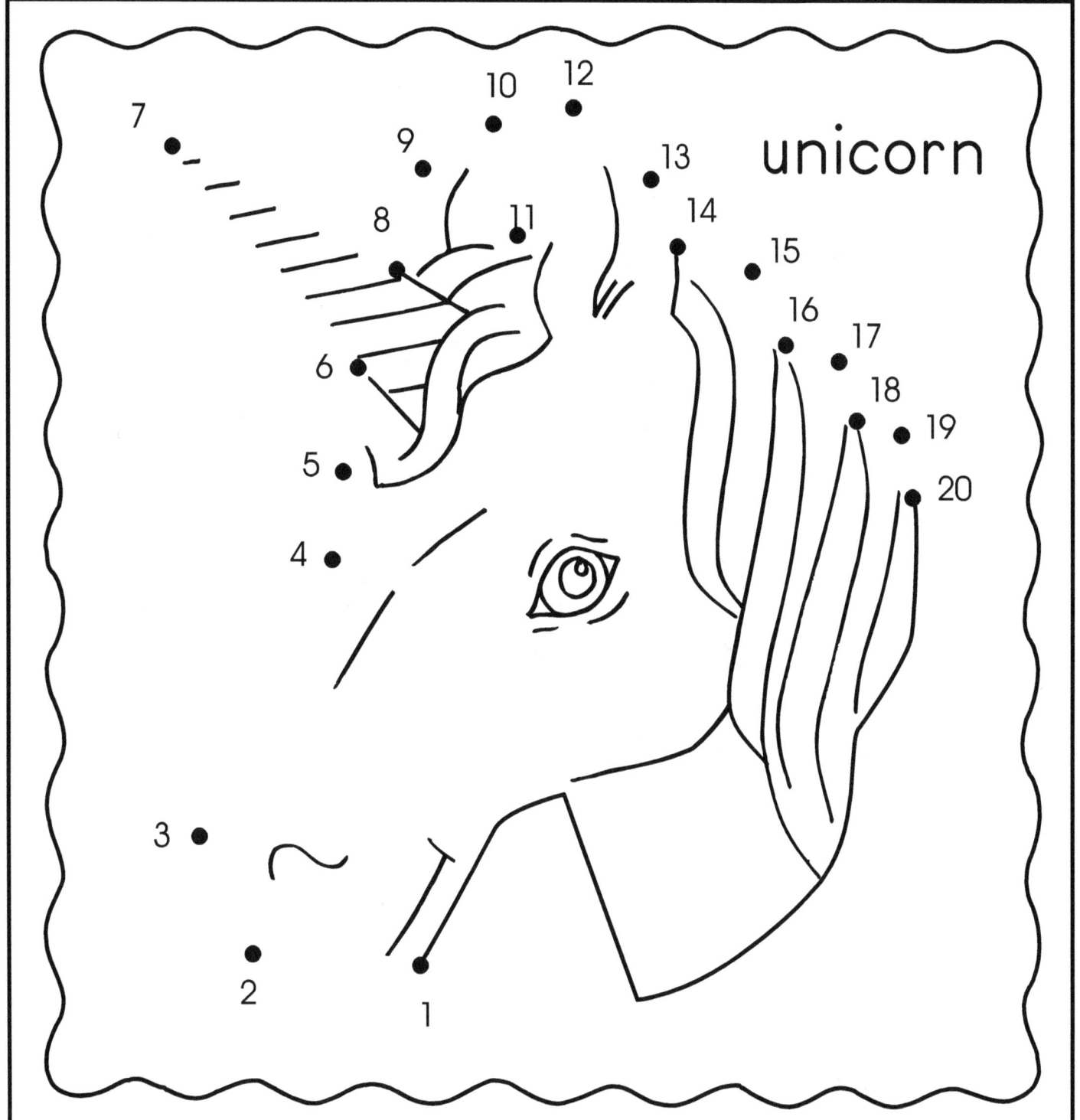

Options:
- Paint on glue then sprinkle glitter on the unicorn's horn.
- Punch two holes, then lace and tie a length of yarn at the top of the cutout to form a hanging picture.

Connect-the-Numbers
Connect Numbers 1 through 20

Start at number **1** to connect the dots. Color the picture.
Cut out and glue the picture on a sheet of construction paper.

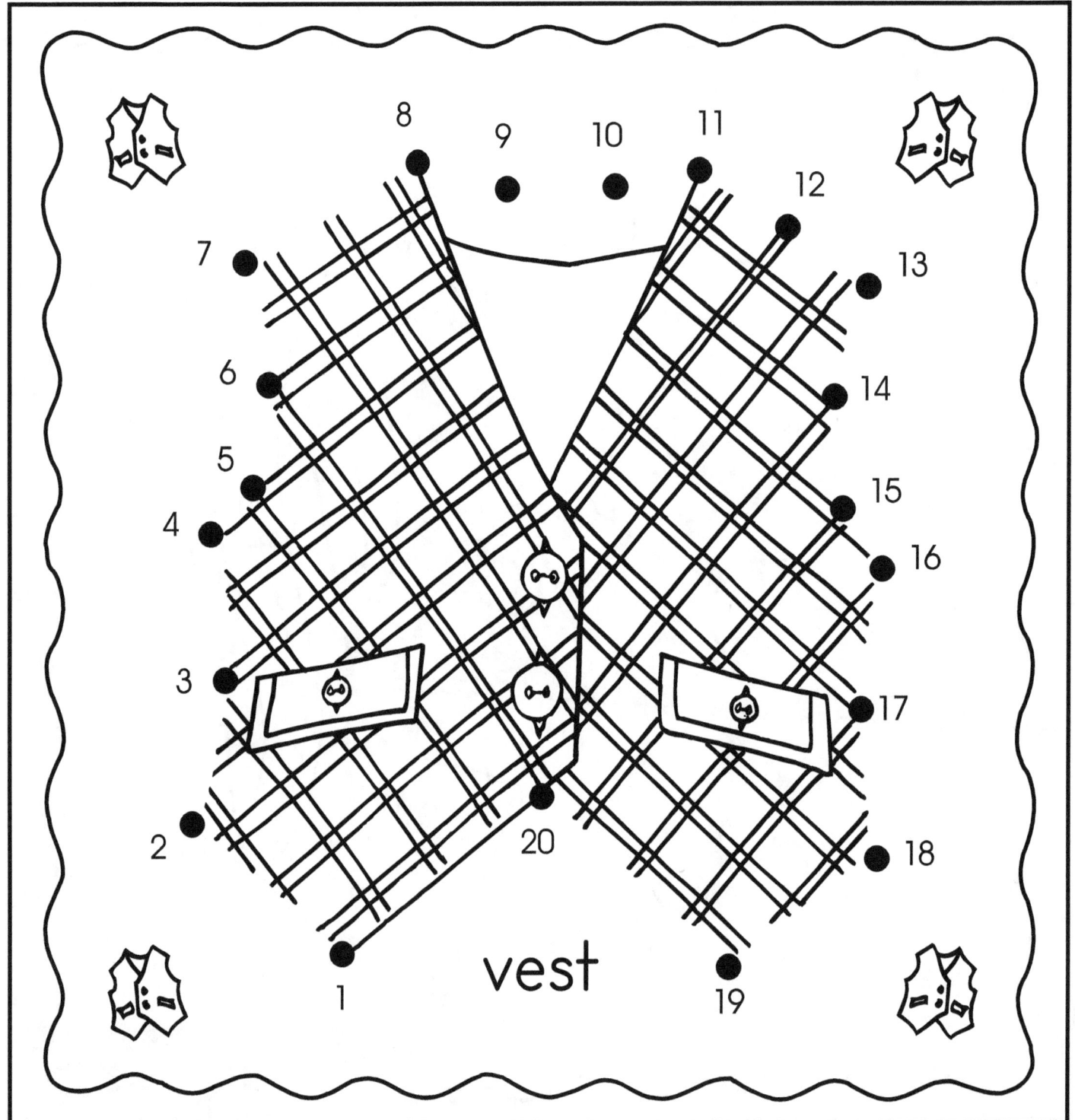

Options:
- Glue buttons on the vest.
- Punch two holes, then lace and tie a length of yarn at the top of the cutout to form a hanging picture.

Connect-the-Numbers
Connect Numbers 1 through 20

Start at number **1** to connect the dots. Color the picture.
Cut out and glue the picture on a sheet of construction paper.

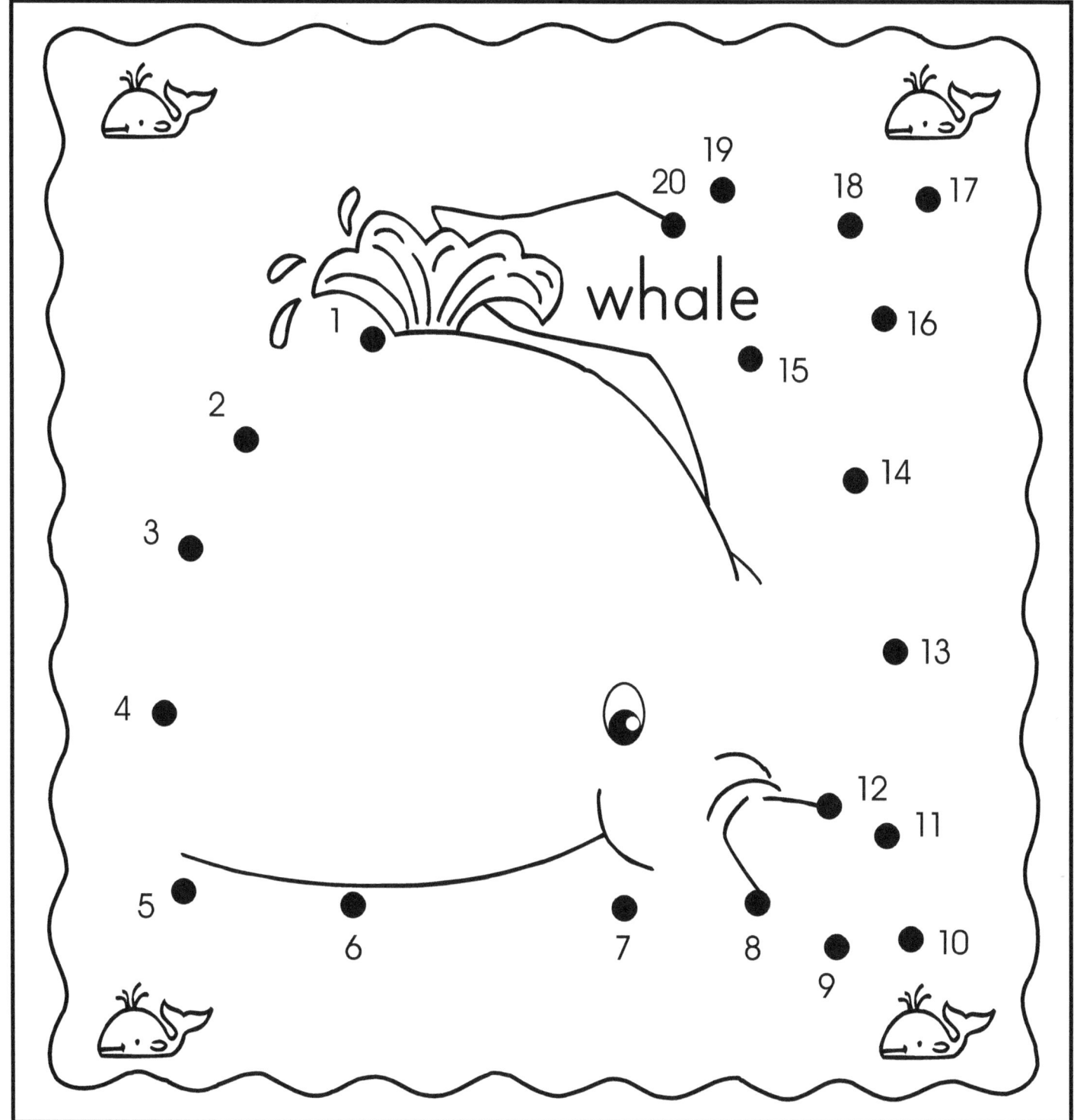

Options:
- Paint the whale with blue watercolor.
- Punch two holes, then lace and tie a length of yarn at the top of the cutout to form a hanging picture.

Scribble Scribble Book Pages

Writing Practice Page

Shapes Page

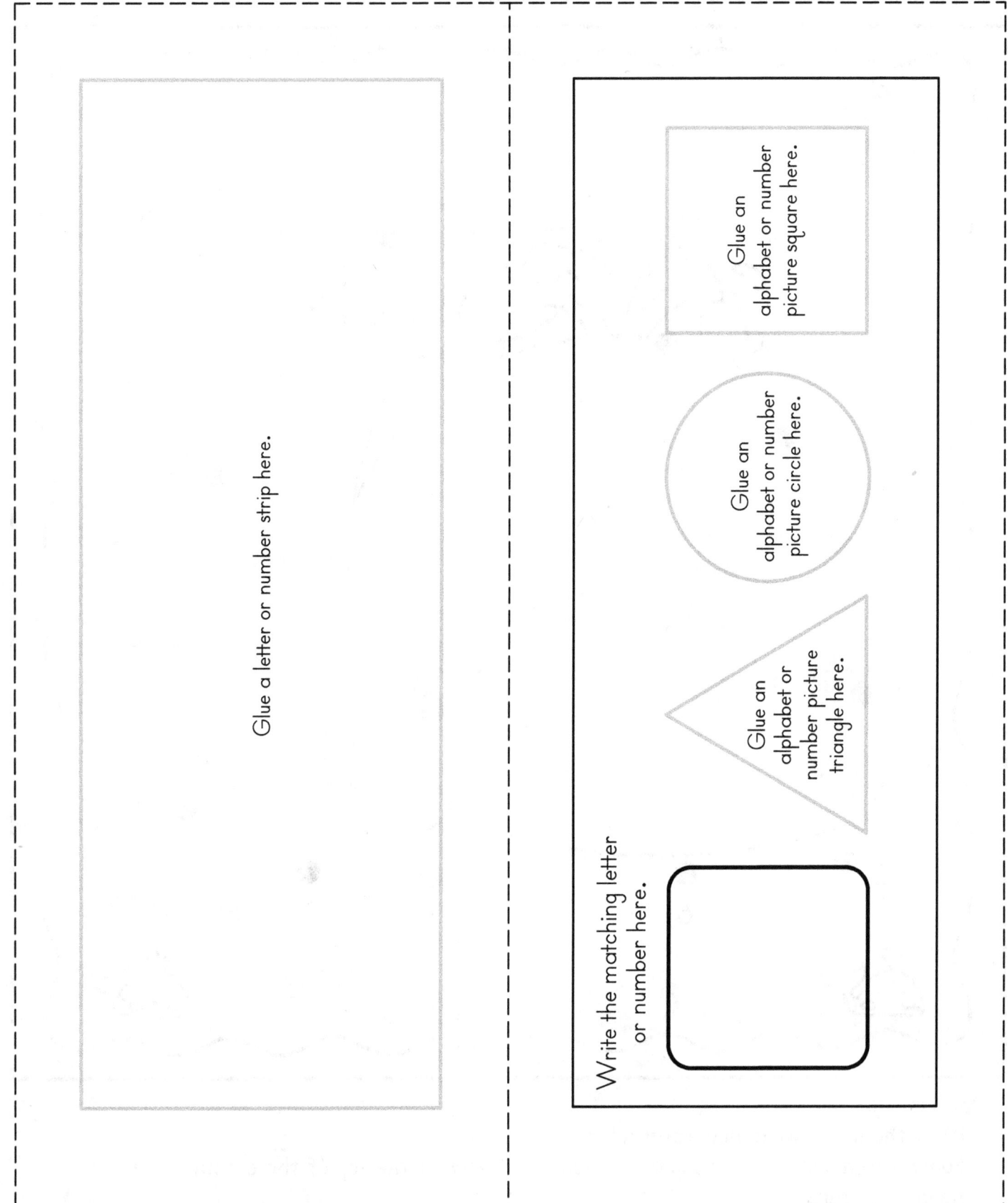

LAB20132 • SCRIBBLE SCRIBBLE • 978-1-937257-19-4   64   ©2013 Little Acorn Books™